Colour

Clash

Intro

The saying that 'red and green should never be seen without a colour in between', has always intrigued me. Red is sometimes replaced by blue in this advice, or orange, or whatever seems to fit for the one giving the colour advice and the situation in front of them. Whatever the context, the phrase refers to the belief that certain colours should not be seen together.

It is possible that the phrase refers to the running lights on ships, which have traditionally been red on one side and green on the other. If another vessel saw green or red lights ahead in the dark, it would mean they were on a collision course. Another theory is that the saying derives from another seafaring tradition, that the hulls of boats should not be painted green in case they became invisible when capsized. However, it's also grounded in colour theory and perhaps the origins of this mantra simply go back to the colour wheel, where red and green sit opposite each other.

Wherever it comes from, I wouldn't pay too much attention to such 'laws'. It's about what feels right for the project in hand, its context and meaning. It's a question of tone and judgment and I love it when designers break with convention and intentionally combine colours that clash and vibrate. Such daring work is still capable of causing a shock to the system. As the images in this book show, breaking the traditional rules about no-go colour combinations is sometimes exactly the right thing to do, if you want to gain attention for your brand and stand out from the crowd.

Colour is fundamental to our experience of the world around us. The human eye can, apparently, perceive over 2.8 million different colours and so it has been suggested that the number of possible colour combinations is virtually infinite. As such, I feel it would be a shame to be too locked in to the conventions of colour theory. Beauty is definitely in the eye of the beholder and wouldn't it be boring if we were all the same?

This book showcases graphic design projects without safe, traditional colour schemes and everyday palettes. With more than 30 international design companies and interviews with acclaimed professionals, we hope it will provide inspiration for anyone wishing to create exciting, even daring, identities using colour.

Colour is one of the essential elements of design. It can help give a project personality and warmth, it can express emotion and communicate messages in an unconscious and subtle way. It can keep, or even navigate, the viewer's interest, drawing the eye; or it can help make elements stand out.

Colour theory is an entire body of practical guidance to colour mixing and the visual effects of specific colour combinations. However, it can be simply seen through the colour wheel, which separates colours into primary, secondary and tertiary terms. We are taught about colour theory in school but many seem to possess an innate sense of it and are aware when colours are used in a harmonious way, or not, regardless of education.

The understanding of such theory dates back to antiquity. Aristotle (d. 322 BCE) and Claudius Ptolemy (d. 168 CE) addressed how colours could be produced by mixing other colours. However, it was only in 1704 that the idea of the primary colours of red, yellow and blue and secondary colours of green, orange and purple appeared when Newton wrote about his Spectrum in 'Opticks'. From there it developed as an independent artistic tradition. White and black were no longer considered colours and an order was imposed on the relationship between complementary colours. Complementary colours were pairs, sitting opposite each other on the colour wheel – for example, blue and orange or red and green. Such colours were found to resonate strongly with each other.

Some theorists and artists today believe juxtaposition of complementary colours produces a strong contrast and a sense of visual tension. Meanwhile, colours next to each other on the wheel model (analogous colours) are seen to produce a single-hued or monochromatic colour experience and give a feeling of harmony together, such as a combination of red with orange or green with yellow.

It's the colours opposite each other that we are most interested in exploring in this book, the ones that really pop together like blue with orange, or deep green with pink accents. These combinations are what people often call a 'colour clash', as they are bright and offer a high contrast, but they do go together and create a great scheme, so the term can be somewhat misleading.

Technically a colour clash is not a particular colour against another colour, it's differing shades of colours that work less well together. For instance, a bright, clear yellow will work well with a strong purple, but less well with a warm, muted purple as the tones will be different. So, if you are going bright, go all in.

Designers today apply the terms 'complementary' and 'clashing' in a looser manner than in the strict colour theory sense. So complementary colours at full strength can be said to clash badly or complement each other. If they can be referred to as 'contrasting', 'complementary' or 'clashing' – then it shows quite how subjective colour combinations can be.

Whatever you want to call them, these colours tend to draw the eye due to their contrast and high energy.

Many people simply avoid using bright colours as they worry they won't work well together but using high contrast colours that potentially clash in design is not necessarily a bad idea. We are naturally compelled to notice saturated colours. It could be argued that saturated colours look ripe and the reason that we respond to them is part of our evolutionary history. They demand attention wherever they appear.

The passing of judgement on certain colour combinations is common across the visual arts. In the past, I've been warned against pink and red – the mother of all colour clashes – blue and red, purple and red, pink and green or green and red – the list goes on. But if you're brave, and willing to experiment, these colours will work together beautifully, without reminding you of Father Christmas or even Freddy Krueger, in the case of the latter – two very contrasting images in themselves.

Contrast is a beautiful thing. When it is done well, even a few bold colours together can work. Creating harmony often depends on the amount of colour used and how closely contrasting colours appear together on the page or screen. Designs with too much clashing colour, too close together may appear to vibrate and overwhelm the viewer, so be warned, it's something that needs experimentation and it is best to steer clear of some colour combinations where text is involved. Making anything hard to read on a printed piece or web page may be contrary to what you are trying to accomplish. Or perhaps that's the desired effect, who am I to judge? It's all about context and I like to challenge people too. Colour pairings are concepts that move with the times and this design book offers a time capsule of the current trends and styles.

This book shows that designers today understand colour harmony but choose to break established rules by mixing unpredictable combinations together, resulting in fresh and fun outcomes. If you can think of a colour combination it's probably in here, proving that anything goes.

In compiling 'Colour Clash', we weren't looking for perfect, harmonious palettes but combinations that surprised, engaged, challenged and grabbed our attention – the ones that shouldn't work but just do. They are palettes that have the power to uplift the spirits, stimulate the senses and convey emotion without words. A well-considered colour palette is capable of bringing incredible power to design and the projects showcased in this book are living proof that colour is king.

We hope this book will provide designers with a host of inventive possibilities when it comes to creating their own palettes.

Jon Dowling
Counterprint

'This book showcases graphic design projects without safe, traditional colour schemes and everyday palettes.'

4

Swiss Pop Art

Raffinerie → raffinerie.com
The special exhibition 'Swiss Pop Art' at the Aargauer Kunsthaus presented, for the first time, a comprehensive overview of this important art movement in Switzerland.

The book, designed by Raffinerie, sheds light on the phenomenon beyond the realm of fine art. Extensive visual material and scholarly text contributions convey the period, which was eventful in political, social and artistic terms. Works by Franz Gertsch, Rosina Kuhn, Urs Lüthi, Max Matter, Markus Raetz, and Peter Stämpfli, among others, are shown.

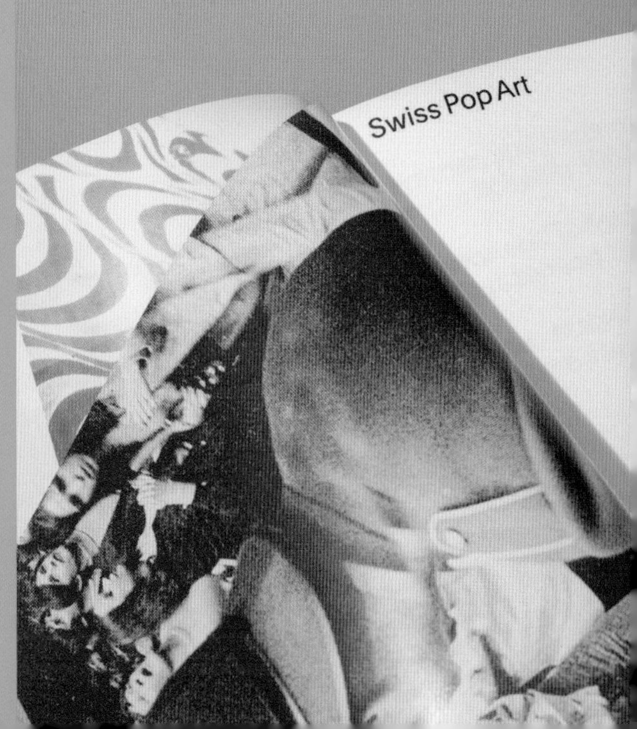

One two three- Vivi for me

VIVI KOLA

G

H

...word ... six times, ... of a roll of wallp... ed down. Karl Gerstn... to promote three washi... 1960s, highlighting the mov... the washing machine for various ... on various kinds of packaging. In a fu... Kola campaign produced by the Kurt Hub... advertising agency in 1967, the entire compo- sition relies on wavy lines which cause the angularity of the letters to disappear. The F12 poster achieves exactly the opposite effect, with the angularity of the monumentally sized word Vivi instead emphasized by the model's curving hips, the slice of lemon, the glass, and the bottle.

Mouths

Images showing the full lips of a woman's mouth are ultimately also a paean to roundness. A number of designers realized this motif in the 1960s and 1970s, as photographs, illustrations, or graphic design. In a 1969 advert for milk by Andy Ziegler the mouth is shown in an unusual position, and typography does great service as an extension of the drinking straw. The Sinalco advert by Peter Emch from 1970 is similar, yet also very different. Almost everything about it is rounded: the full lips, the drinking straw, its hollow form emphasized by slightly curved diagonal stripes, the waisted bottle as part of the product name, and the two other curved lines of text. The background is composed of greatly enlarged yellow Ben-Day dots. Everything about the poster—the red lips motif, the impression of immediacy thanks to the scaling and tight crop, the coloring, the dots, the written text—tells us unmistakably that it is citing the oeuvre of American Pop artist Roy Lichtenstein. A more two-dimensional mouth appears in a 1971 poster by the Josef Müller-Brockmann studio promoting *Die schalkhafte Witwe* for Zurich's opera house. The deliberately irregular contours do, however, create a three-dimensional effect; the red lips are pouting towards the viewer, while the white text on purple ground seems to vanish into the background.

One, two, three — Vivi for me

6

Varieté

Requena → andresrequena.es

The Varieté box, where all Sans & Sans teas are brought together in a dégustation format, has quickly become the emblem of the brand, an object of desire, a coveted symbol, an icon. That is why each new edition is eagerly awaited.

Taking into consideration its positioning and context, each new edition is presented as a blank canvas on which to express the idea of diversity through historical references of culture and art.

In this case Requena took, as a guideline, the idea of colour and its use by the De Stijl artistic movement. Instead of dramatising a flat surface, instead of being a superficial ornamentation, colour is like light, an elemental means of purely architectural expression.

36u.
Varieté
SELECTION OF TEAS AND INFUSIONS
36u.
Varieté
SELECTION OF TEAS AND INFUSIONS
36u.
SELECTION OF TEAS AND INFUSIONS
SELECTION OF TEAS AND INFUSIONS

8

Colección Infusión

Requena → andresrequena.es

The Varieté collection plays with the concept of diversity through the use of colour. For this new Infusión box, Requena aimed to emphasise this same concept, this time adding diversity in its forms.

Inspired by the mixtures that are generated between the different threads and infusions, they tried to decode them in a scenario where geometry coexists, deforms, evolves and merges with organic and even irregular shapes.

Requena wanted these shapes to appeal to sensoriality, emotion, intuition and reflect the sensitive spirit of the product. It is not just a matter of randomly varied shapes, but of harmonious, soft, sensitive elements that interact and relate to each other in the same way as the flavours of each infusion.

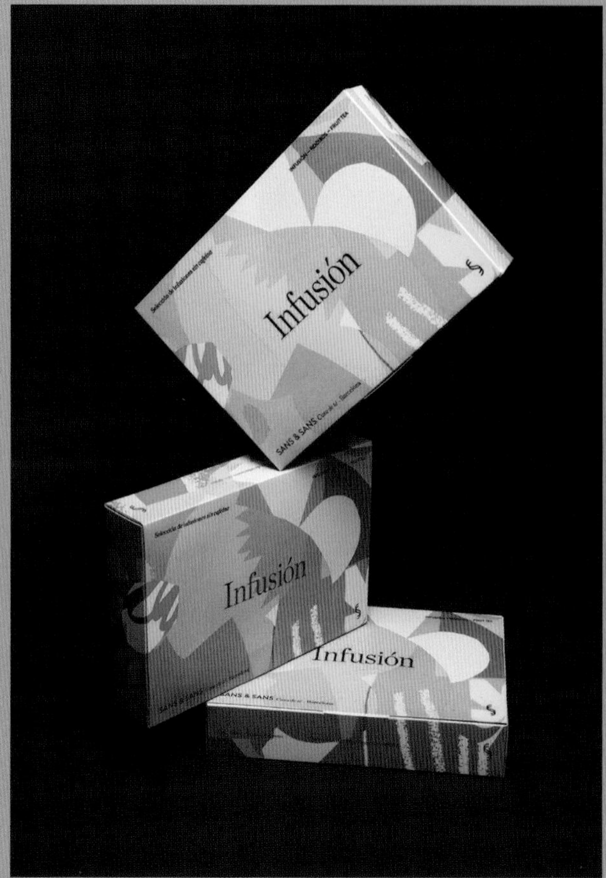

Selección de infusiones sin cafeína
Infusión
SANS & SANS Casa de té · Barcelona

Infusión
Selección de infusiones sin cafeína
INFUSIÓN – ROOIBOS – FRUIT TEA
SANS & SANS Casa de té - Barcelona

11

'The Varieté collection plays with the concept of diversity through the use of colour.'

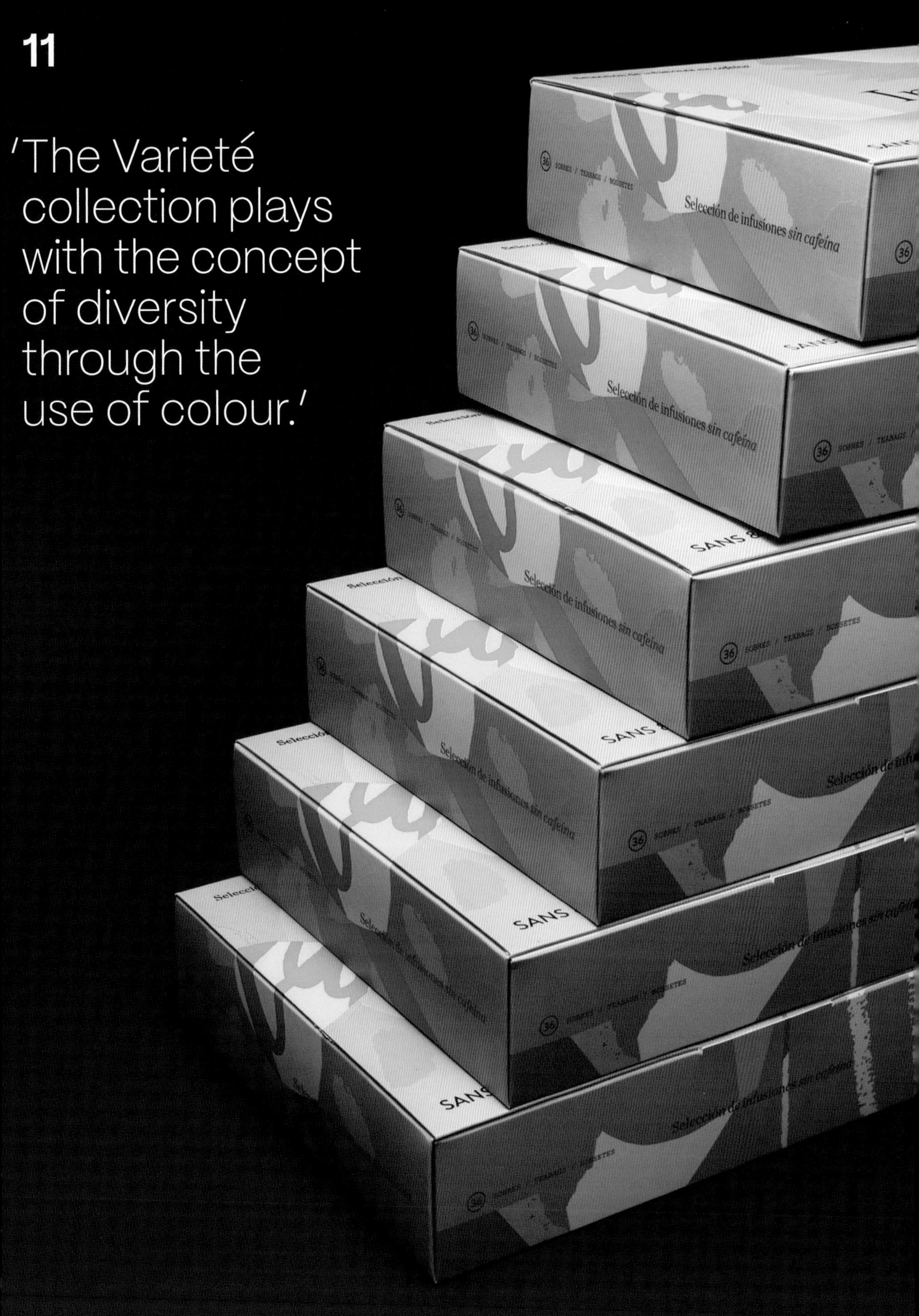

NORWEGIAN FOREST
挪威的森林
URBAN JUNGLE
READING AROMA
你的
伴读香氛
LIGHT OF TAHITI
你的
伴读香氛
READING AROMA
大溪地
之光
DREAM POEMS
SUNSET CITY
君临城的
余晖
你的
伴读香氛
READING AROMA
DREAM POEMS
一半沙漠
一半海水
DREAM POEMS
DESERT AND SEA
你的
伴读香氛
READING AROMA
READING AROMA
你的
伴读香氛
OPERA NIGHT
安达卢西亚
ANDALUSIA
EARL'S ROOM
伯爵的房间
DREAM POEMS
READING AROMA
你的
伴读香氛

13 Information Poster

Simin Xu → behance.net/siminxbs

This product information poster was designed for the 'to Define' store. In the exploration of the visual language, Simin Xu thought about what the design can convey to the user. For example, colours with different attributes can express various emotions of the brand series, so a systematic new colour series was born.

This was combined with eye-catching Chinese typography to help strengthen the recognition of a domestic, high-quality brand.

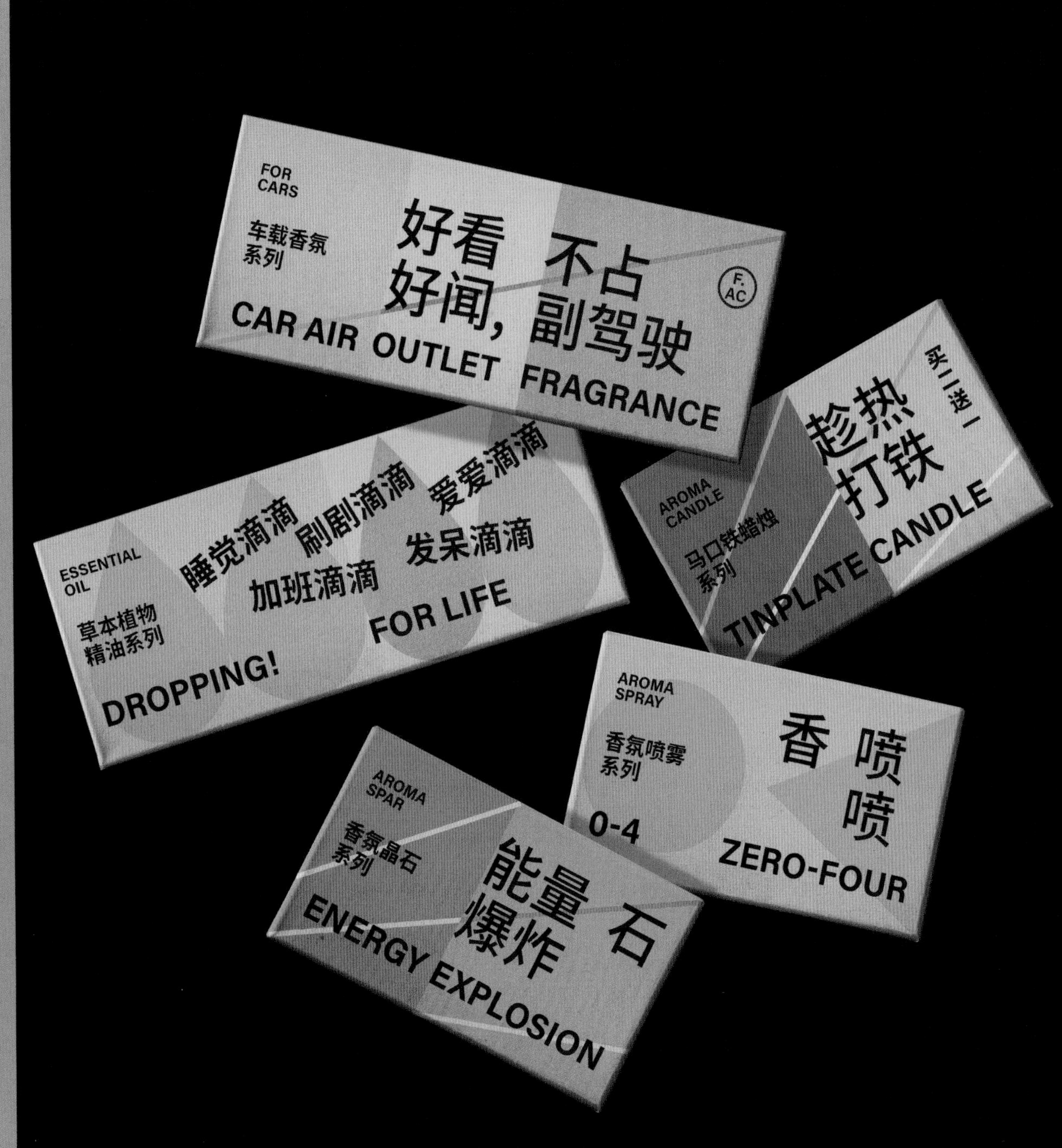

14 Macau Poster Design Association 10th Anniversary Invitational Exhibition

Untitled Macao → untitledmacao.com

Since it was established in 2009, Macau Poster Design Association has been organising poster exhibitions and exhibiting local designers' works not only in Macau, but also in other cities in Asia.

The Association strives to promote Macau's design culture and to facilitate exchanges between the local and international design communities, by actively exploring diverse and innovative exhibition models. To celebrate Macau Poster Design Association's 10th anniversary, Untitled Macao invited designers from around the world to join them and exhibit their posters at this 'Happy Birthday' exhibition.

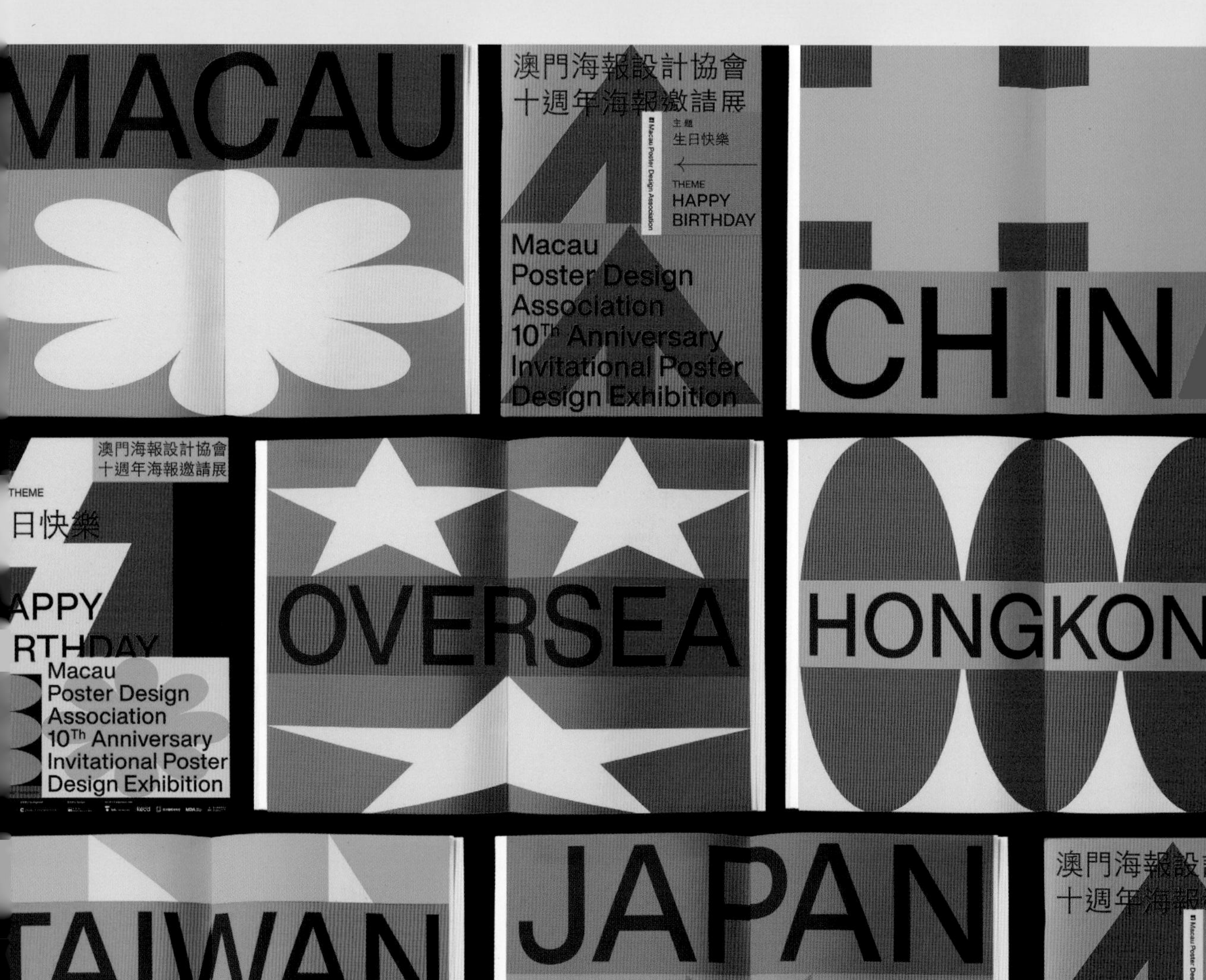

十週年海報邀請展
展覽日期 EXHIBITION DATES
2019 /11 /04—
2019 /11 /12
Macau
主題
生日快樂
THEME
HAPPY
BIRTHDAY
Macau Poster Design Association

澳門海報

十週年海

2019

日快樂

ME

APPY

IRTH

計協會
邀請展
DESIGNED BY / AU CHON HIN@UNTITLED
1/04-2019/11
Maca
Post esign
Assoc on
0Th A versar
nvita al Post
Design Exhibiti

18 FCAC Summer—2021

Play On Play → playonplaystudio.com

Play On Play (POP) Studio were asked to brand the 2021 Footscray Community Arts Center (FCAC) summer festival. Marketed under the umbrella 'FCAC Summer', the program included four weeks of live music, kid's experiences, creative workshops, visual arts, and talks.

The concept was guided by the festival's tagline 'Art in Your Backyard'. Strong references were taken from the exquisite colours found in Australia's native flora and natural landscape. More specifically, the red desert, koalas, and bottlebrush flowers. The design showcases a bright, bold palette using minimalist graphic motifs to achieve a naive but playful visual identity.

FCAC
SUMMER
ART IN
YOUR
BACKYARD
JAN 22—FEB 21

FCAC
SUMMER
Bluestone
Sessions
JAN 23
FCAC
SUMMER
Simon Sisay
SO.Crates
Empat Lima
DJ: Mike Gurrieri
Bluestone
Sessions
JAN 23

FCAC
SUMMER

FOOTSCRAY
COMMUNITY
ARTS
CENTRE
ART IN
YOUR
BACKYARD
JAN 22—FEB 21

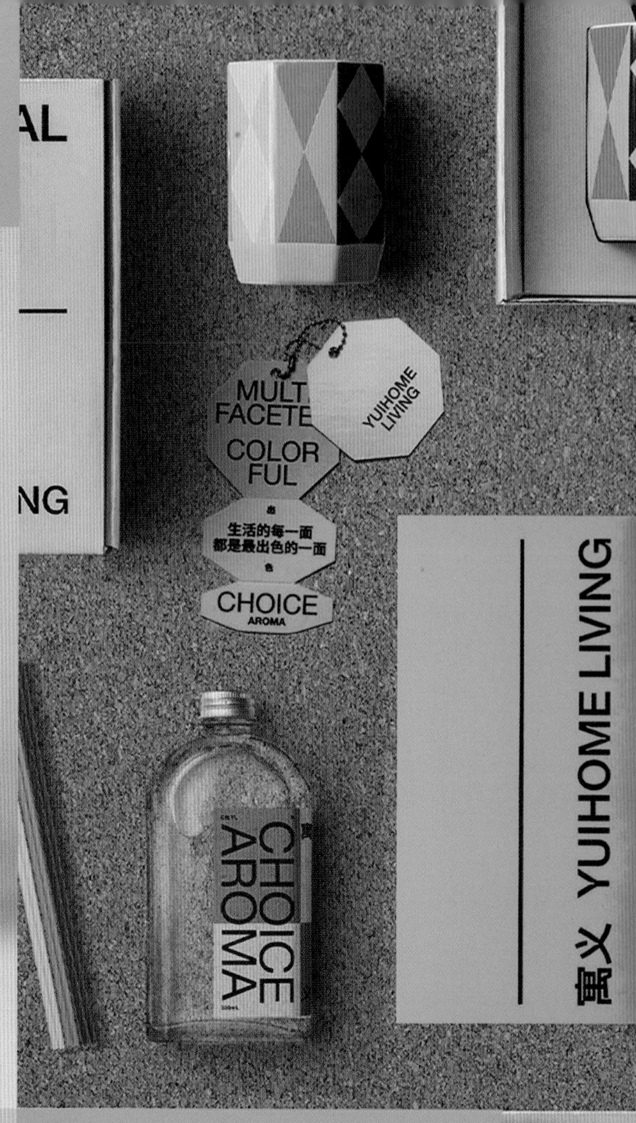

寓义 to Define

Simin Xu → behance.net/siminxbs

This home fragrance packaging design is for 寓义 to Define. The product consists of a bottled liquid and a diffuser container. The collection is titled 'Excellent' and aims to express the best of every aspect of life.

Polyhedrons and colour elements are incorporated into the overall packaging design. The octagon is reflected in the shape and packaging, while all graphic design and material choices revolve around colour.

This is a new experiment in home fragrance design, exploring the possibility of communication between products and people.

'This is a new experiment in home fragrance design, exploring the possibility of communication between products and people.'

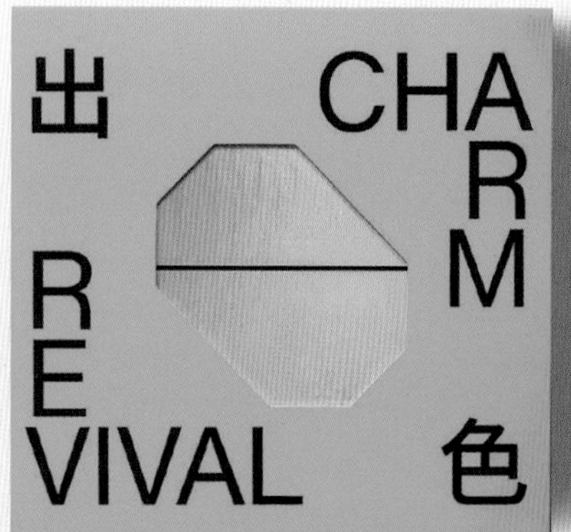
出
CHA
R
M
RE
VIVAL
色

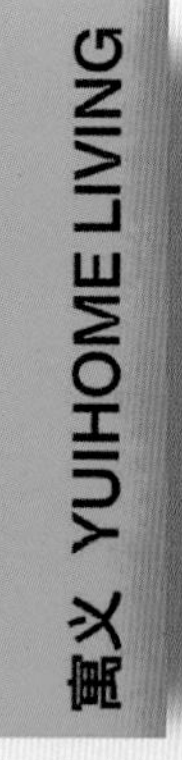
寓义 YUIHOME LIVING

CHARM
REVIVAL
©YUIHOME LIVING

DIFFUSED
VASE
CHARM
REVIVAL
©YUIHOME LIVING

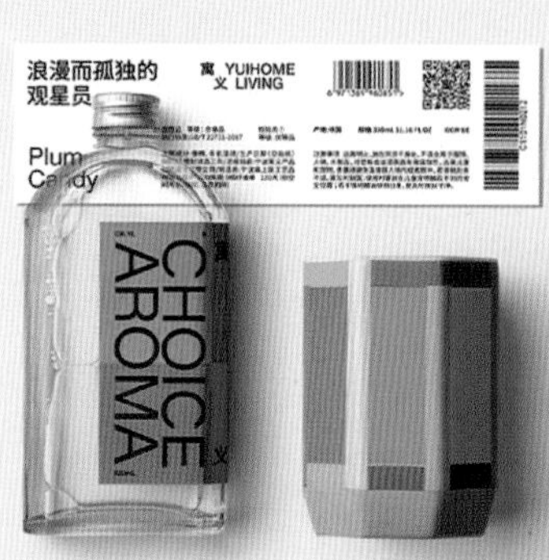
浪漫而孤独的
观星员
寓 YUIHOME
义 LIVING
Plum
Candy
CHOICE
AROMA
寓
义

寓
WHITE TEA
义

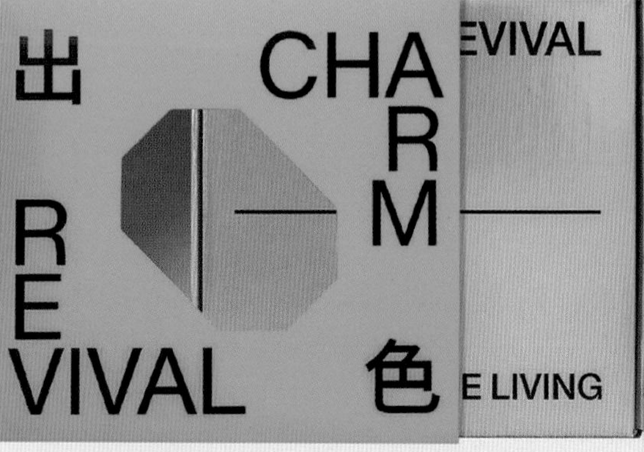
出
CHA
R
M
RE
VIVAL
色
EVIVAL
E LIVING

CHOICE
AROMA
寓
义
BLUE RAINDROP
330mL
寓
义
PLUM CANDY
330mL
寓
义
CHIBA ROSE
330mL
寓
义
WHITE TEA
330mL
寓
义
JUNIPER BERRY
330mL

CHOICE AROMA
RAINDROP
CHOICE AROMA
CHIBA
JUNIPER BERRY
CHOICE AROMA

MULT
FACETE
COLOR
FUL
出
生活的每一面
都是最出色的一面
色
CHOICE
AROMA
YUIHOME
LIVING

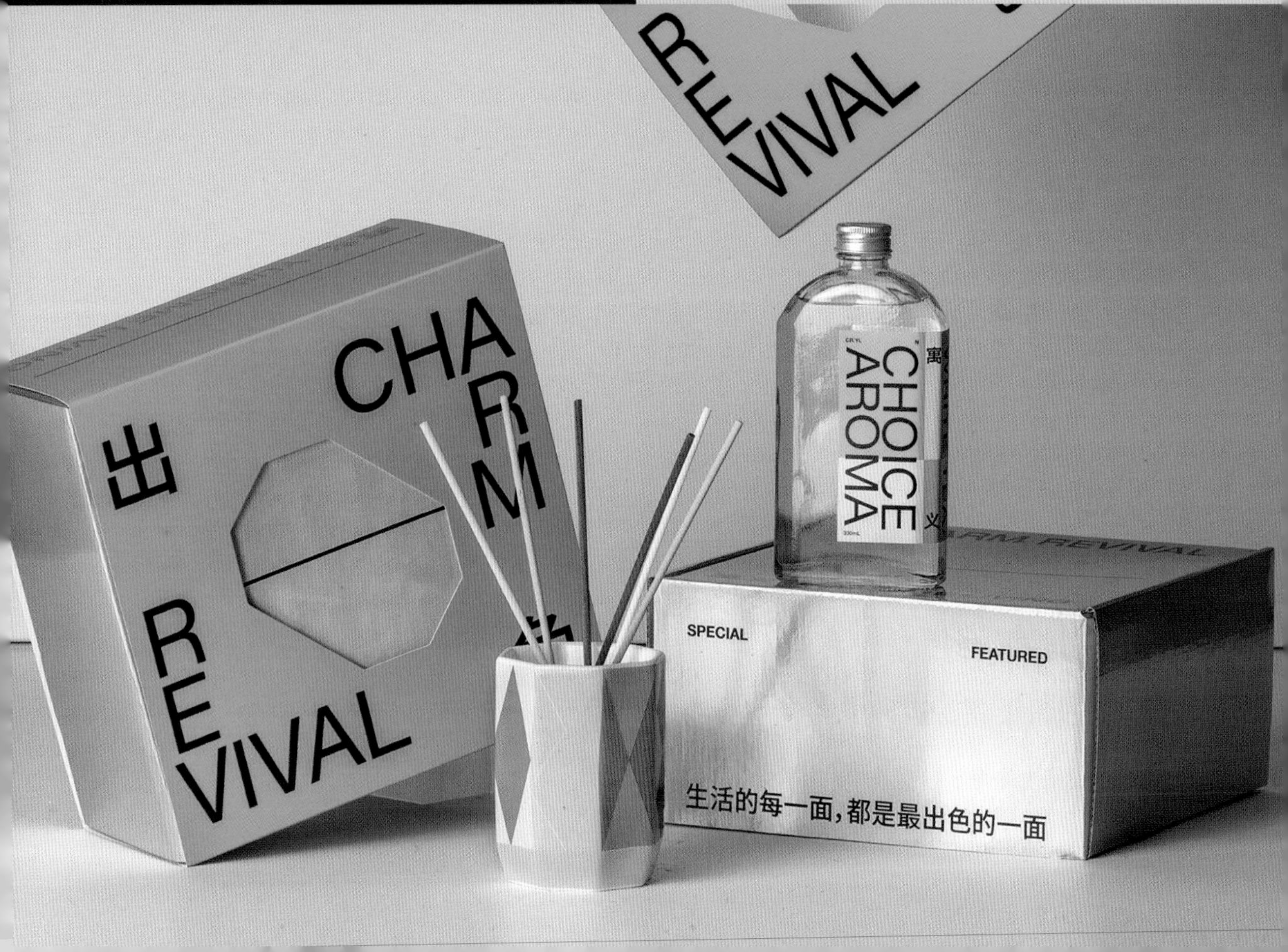

RE
VIVAL
CHA
R
M
出
RE
VIVAL
CHOICE
AROMA
SPECIAL
FEATURED
生活的每一面,都是最出色的一面

Cheng Peng

Interview 01

Cheng Peng is a graphic designer and illustrator based in Shenzhen, China. Her works, combining abstract geometry and colour, often focus on typography, illustration and poster design.

→ behance.net/kabaopeng

What is your background and how did you become involved in graphic design?

I love graphics and colours. I often marvel at the great variety of wonderful graphics there can be in the world: graphics in nature or within traditional culture, for example, which inspire me so much during my life and creative work. In return, I want to visualise what I see and what I think through the employment of combining graphics and colours.

What are you driven by creatively?

I'm inspired by subtle feelings and observations from my daily life, and more fundamentally, my love for life always serves as the source of my inspiration. Sometimes inspiration can be fragile and easily fleating in memory, so I choose to express and keep these observations by using wonderful graphics.

How important is colour to your work?

I believe there are profound connections between graphics and colours. Adjusting the proportions and combinations of these two has given my designs infinite possibilities. Additionally, sometimes words alone may not be able to convey thoughts and emotions properly, but colours may find the niche and reach further and deeper in terms of expression. This is why I find colour so attractive.

How do you stop your personal preferences getting in the way of what is required for the client?

I prefer the combination of different colours rather than a single and particular colour because combining colours together always makes the work more impressive and personal. As to commercial projects, the client would usually ask to avoid using the brand colours of their competitors, but I consider the colour requirements as helpful guidelines rather than limitations. I start by crafting around the available colours, and try to find the best combination and contrast to achieve unique and desired results. Fortunately, I don't find any colours unattractive.

How important is harmony within your colour palettes? Is it always necessary?

Harmony, or to be more specific, whether combining different colours together can bring a sense of visual beauty, is always of great importance to me. When I used to use colours, I focused on the hue itself, to see whether certain hues match harmoniously. But during one of my creative processes, I attempted to change the saturation and lightness of the colours and combined them together, the result brought me a new perception of colour, which I think is also a kind of harmony.

Do you have a favourite designer or artist for their use of colour and why?

I am a huge fan of Malika Favre. She often shares the colour combinations she finds in her life on social media, and most of the combinations are highly saturated and pleasant. I believe there is a certain connection between her work and her daily observation of colours, and I am somehow connected to her observations and I can feel her love for life.

Do you have a process for selecting a colour palette for a client?

I will first ask the client what they expect from the visual experience of the work. For example, some clients want to present a warm atmosphere, others want to present a professional and reliable brand perception, and some clients want to present ethnic or exotic characteristics. Then, I start to combine my colour palette according to the clients' key words of feelings, perceptions, etc.

How can an effective colour palette enhance a brand's identity?

Colours, as well as graphics, can bring uniqueness to a brand. Different colours have different characteristics, affecting the audiences' emotions. So first of all, the perception that a brand wants convey to the customers has to be made very clear. For example, Uniqlo uses red and white to convey its message visually, efficiently and clearly. The contrast between IKEA's brand colours of yellow and blue gives people a professional and reliable visual feeling. Instagram uses pink, purple, yellow and other high-saturation and bright colours that blend together in a gradient form to bring people a young, diverse and inclusive sense of openness. Defining the 'character' of the brand by using monochromatic, contrasting, complementary or other combinations of colours are just some of the methods to help deliver a unique brand image.

What are your goals over the coming years?

Of course I will continue to explore the possibilities between graphics and colours to the best of my ability for the years to come. In addition, I have recently become obsessed with traditional Chinese culture, especially the shape and colour combinations of traditional patterns which have inspired me a lot. As a result, I would also like to create some design works concerning traditional Chinese culture in the future.

超越幸福
2022

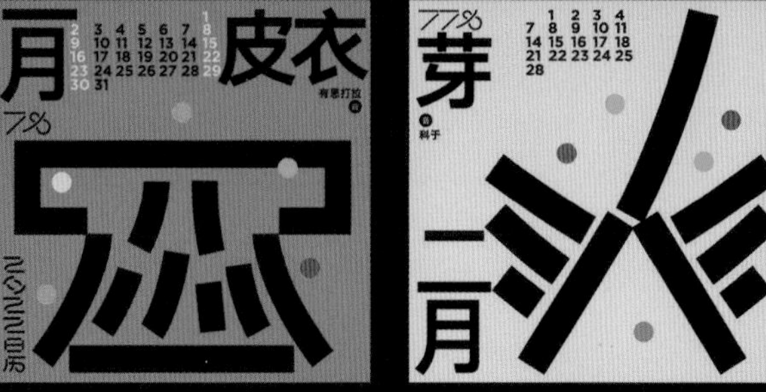

DONGBA New Year Gift Box

Cheng Peng → behance.net/kabaopeng
This gift box includes a New Year's calendar, a set of door stickers and New Year paintings (traditional Chinese New Year folkart, to put up on doors and windows). The inspiration came from traditional Chinese culture – Dongba literature.

Dongba is the language used by the Naxi people of eastern Tibet and northern Yunnan in China and is the only pictographic character still alive in the world. Cheng Peng reinterperated it, inspired by its aesthetics, in the hope to convey the charm of the 'new' traditional Chinese culture in this work.

ift Box
门贴
Folk

年画

Happy
New
Year

Calendar

Folk Art

17

modular und frei rollbar durch den Raum

vorzügliches Lebenskonzept: Leichtigkeit

dünne Schiebetüren gleiten leise und platzsparend

Benny Mosimann

Ellipsetower

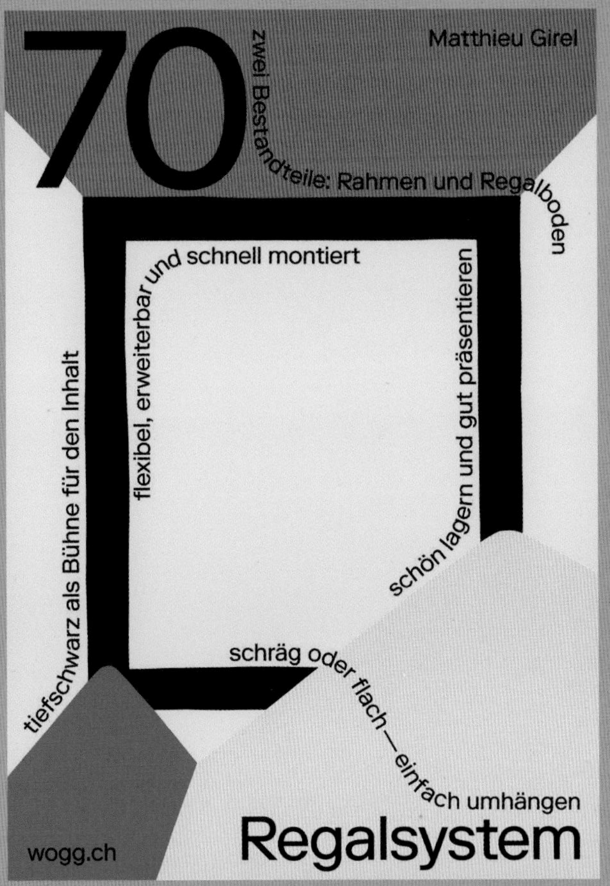

70
Matthieu Girel
zwei Bestandteile: Rahmen und Regalboden
und schnell montiert
flexibel, erweiterbar
schön lagern und gut präsentieren
tiefschwarz als Bühne für den Inhalt
schräg oder flach—einfach umhängen
wogg.ch
Regalsystem

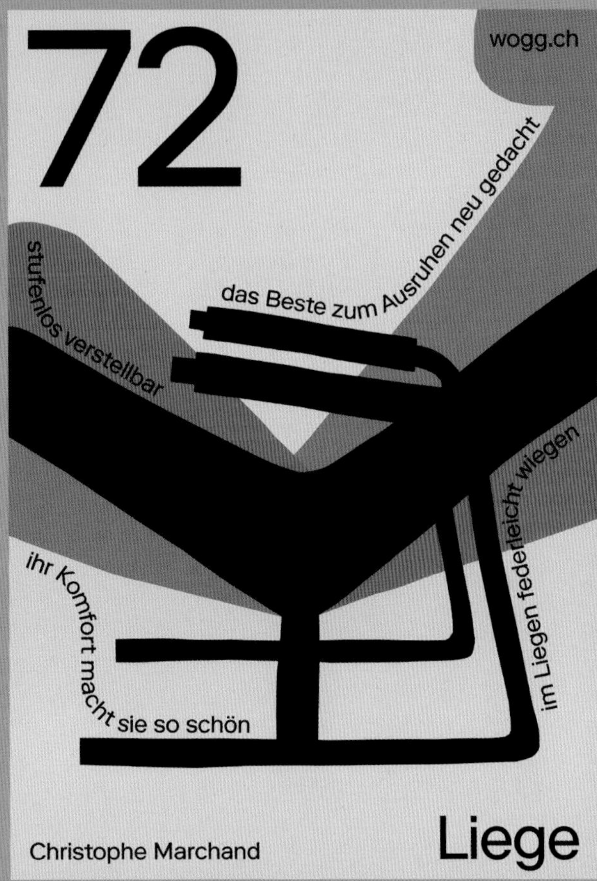

72
wogg.ch
das Beste zum Ausruhen neu gedacht
stufenlos verstellbar
im Liegen federleicht wiegen
ihr Komfort macht sie so schön
Christophe Marchand
Liege

WOGG Poster Series

Badesaison → badesaison.ch
This five-part poster series was created with the innovative Swiss design furniture manufacturer WOGG. Each poster portrays a highlight from the extensive collection.

The intention is to interpret the main feature of the furniture illustratively. In addition, there is the textual level, which fluidly adapts to the shapes. The posters could be screen printed – this enabled Badesaison to reproduce the very intense and vivid colours optimally.

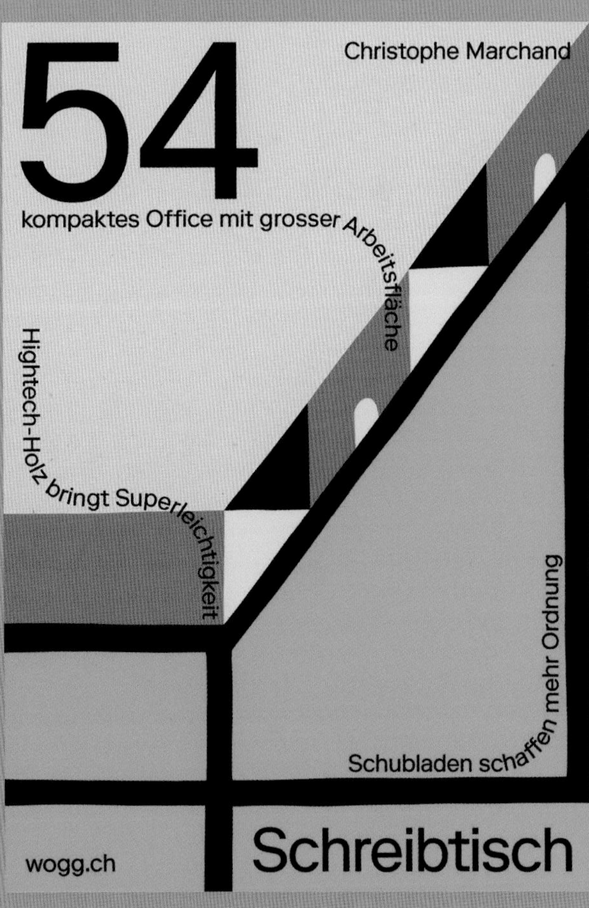

54
Christophe Marchand
kompaktes Office mit grosser Arbeitsfläche
Hightech-Holz bringt Superleichtigkeit
Schubladen schaffen mehr Ordnung
wogg.ch
Schreibtisch

Be Water Soap

B&W Graphic Lab → behance.net/BWLAB
The Be Water Soap brand was founded to provide customised cleaning for sensitive skin. The delicate foam brings a more gentle cleaning process. To reflect this, B&W add a cheerful aesthetic to the brand and its packaging material. It's futuristic appearance breaks with the conventional, simple style of design in the existing in the industry.

BE WATER SOAP
SHORT SPA
RECYCL
PALNT-BASED
FINER FOAM CLEANS SENSITIVE SKIN, RETAINS CERTAIN MOISTURE AND CLEANS DIRT FROM EACH PORE, KEEPS A MILD FRAGRANCE FOR A LONG TIME, AND REDUCES AIR POLLUTION FROM THE OUTSIDE
FRESH 24 MONTHS AFTER FIRST USE
100%
BE WATER SOAP

BE WATER SOAP
SHORT SPA

90g
BE WATER SOAP
SHORT SPA

90g
BE WATER SOAP
SHORT SPA

90g
BE WATER SOAP
SHORT SPA

90g
BE WATER SOAP
SHORT SPA

SHORT
90g
BE WATER SOA
B&W LAB IS A MULTI
UNIQUE GRAPHIC STYL
PACKAGE DESIGN AND
PROJECTS, CREATING

B&W Graphic Lab
BE WATER
B&W LAB IS A MULTIDISCIPLINARY GRAPHIC DESIGN STUDIO, BASED ON UNIQUE GRAPHIC STYLE, BRANDING AND MARKET ANALYSIS. SPECIALIZED IN PACKAGE DESIGN AND BRAND IDENTITY, WE HAVE WORKED ON NUMEROUS PROJECTS, CREATING INSPIRING DESIGN AND RESULTS INTO THE MARKET.

HAPPY
NEW
YEAR

BONNE
ANNÉE

The Year of the Tiger Poster Series

Cheng Peng → behance.net/kabaopeng
Cheng Peng created this series of posters to celebrate the Lunar New Year of the Tiger. They used green, blue, orange and rose, which are often utilised in traditional Chinese folk art. Cheng Peng wanted to incorporate these traditional colours in their work, so that they can be reborn with a new life.

HAPPY
NEW
YEAR
BONNE
ANNÉE
虎

HAPPY
NEW
YEAR

HAPPY
NEW
YEAR

Soochi

Ima Creative → imacreative.studio
Soochi supplement drinks merge the science of nature, taste and innovation to deliver on functional benefits for the skin, body and mind, with added collagen, vitamins and prebiotics. Pronounced 'Soo-chee' and derived from the Latin word 'Suci', - meaning 'juice'/'nectar of life', the bold colour palette communicates this idea of sweetness, nectar and vitality. The Soochi woman, housed inside an arched shape (a shape synonymous as a symbol for rebirth), honours the fruits of wellness and provides a visual hint to each flavour's fresh and fruity ingredients.

Photography: Kindred Studio

Verisol® Collagen + Prebiotic Soda
SOOCHI
Verisol® Collagen + Prebiotic Soda
SOOCHI
SOOCHI

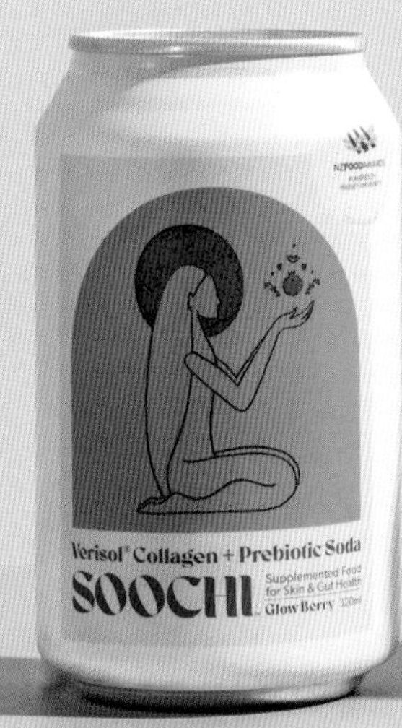
Verisol® Collagen + Prebiotic Soda
SOOCHI
Supplemented Food for Skin & Gut Health
Glow Berry

Verisol® Collagen + Prebiotic Soda
SOOCHI
Supplemented Food for Skin & Gut Health
Passion Peach

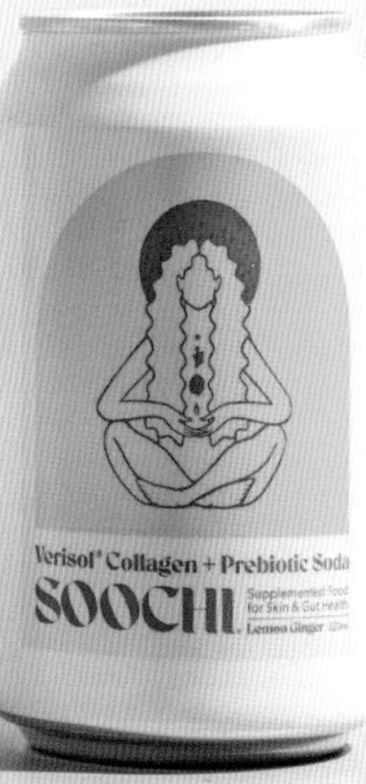
Verisol® Collagen + Prebiotic Soda
SOOCHI
Supplemented Food for Skin & Gut Health
Lemon Ginger

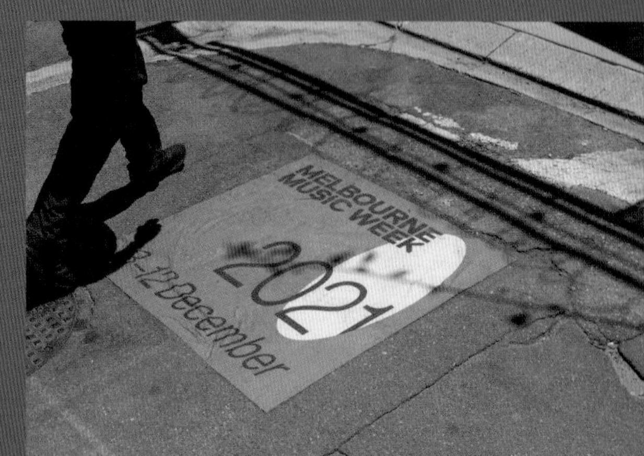
MELBOURNE
MUSIC WEEK
2021
3–12 December

MELBOURNE
MUSIC WEEK
2021
3–12 December
SHOUSE
Sleep D
Pinch Points
SHOUSE, Georgia Maq,
Holly Herndon, Carl Cox,
Luke Howard, Sleep D,
Kardajala Kirridarra, Andras,
Emma Donovan & The Putbacks,
PINCH POINTS, Bananagun,
Ruby Savage, BUMPY, Terry,
Soju Gang, C.FRIM, dj pgz,
Simona Castricum, Press Club,
Billy Davis, Dallas Woods,
IN2STELLAR, Female Wizard,
Jordan Dennis, CLAMM,
LUCIANBLOMKAMP, daine,
Jennifer Loveless + More

Melbourne Music Week—2021

Play On Play → playonplaystudio.com

Now in its second decade, Melbourne Music Week (MMW) continues to play a crucial role as one of the largest festivals supporting and promoting the city's world-renowned music scene.

Play On Play (POP) were commissioned to create a fresh visual identity for the 2021 festival centered around the theme of 'emerging'. After surviving one of the longest lockdowns in the world, Melbourne and its thriving music scene were due to re-open at the end of 2021. Behaving as a motif, the date and oval represent the re-opening of the city, with the text emerging from the unknown grey area into a bright and colourful future.

Melbourne Music Week has pre-established brand guidelines where purple is the hero colour. The brief for 2021 called for a new and ultimately different brand direction that showcased Melbourne's cultural diversity and appealed to a larger demographic. To achieve an unusual palette, Play On Play drew colour inspiration from current runway fashion and artists such as Josef Albers and Rothko.

Photography: Josh Robenstone

'To achieve an unusual palette, Play On Play drew colour inspiration from current runway fashion and artists such as Josef Albers and Rothko.'

MELBOURNE
MUSIC WEEK
3–12 December
JCDecaux
YOUNG AND JACKSON
HOTEL
YOUNG & JACKSON
METRO TUNNEL
WATCH
FOR
TRAMS

2021
JCDecaux
1875
JACKSON
CHLOE'S
NO ENTRY
AUTHORISED VEHICLES EXCEPTED
BICYCLES EXCEPTED
ROAD WORK AHEAD
PREPARE TO STOP

115–119 Wallis Road

Marlon Tate → marlontate.com

Located in the heart of Hackney Wick, London's industrial district turned cultural and creative hub, 115–119 Wallis Road is a property development and regeneration project consisting of affordable workspaces, retail and apartment buildings proposed and designed by Pollard Thomas Edwards.

Facing the challenge of convincing the sceptical local community of the project's necessity, as well as raising awareness of its regenerative aspirations, famed creative agency Marlon Tate was brought in to create its visual identity, strategy and communications.

Inspired by Hackney Wick's transition from industry to creativity, the agency decided to establish the regeneration as a 'cultural moment'. Intentionally avoiding any of the slickness typical to new developments, Marlon Tate's solution instead builds upon Hackney Wick's plethora of music festival posters and their bold repetition of colour. The resulting identity system revolves around purposely straightforward and lo-fi elements; those primarily being horizontal stripes in an unusual combination of brown and blue. "We immersed ourselves within a 'back-to-basics' mindset," says Marlon Tate's founder and Creative Director Nikos Georgopoulos, explaining that they were recreating a "kind of music festival excitement," where not worrying too much about legibility, was all part of the plan.

'Intentionally avoiding any of the slickness typical to new developments, Marlon Tate's solution instead builds upon Hackney Wick's plethora of music festival posters and their bold repetition of colour.'

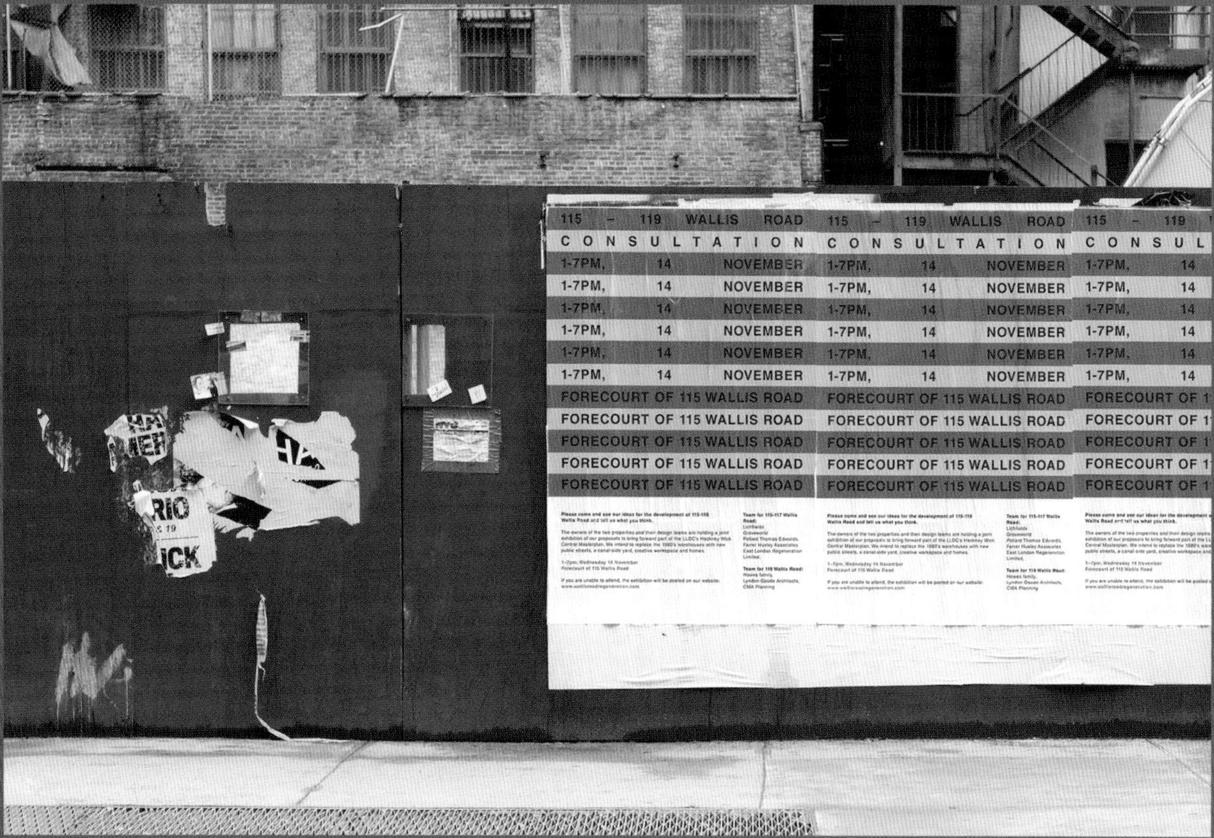

Denada

Jo Cutri Studio → jocutristudio.com
Denada translates to 'It's Nothing' so like the product itself the design is stripped back of any additives. The ingredients are all natural with no surprises and the packaging reflects the same philosophy. Something minimal, yet sophisticated.

Throughout the design process Jo Cutri Studio always gave consideration to how the entire range looked on the shelf together and not just as individual tubs. This stemmed from being a new product and needing a point of difference to have some impact in the marketplace.

Inspiration and research covered everything from modern interior colour design trends to retro Japanese medical packaging.

Photography: Simone Ruggiero – instagram.com/sim0ner

denada™
sugar free 98.5%
caramel macadamia ice cream
low carb. no added sugar. all natural 475ml
denada™
sugar free 98.5%
caramel macadamia ice cream
low carb. no added sugar. all natural 475ml
denada™
sugar free 98.5%
caramel macadamia ice cream
low carb. no added sugar. all natural 475ml

denada™
sugar free 98.8%
salted caramel vegan ice cream
denada™
sugar free 99.2%
vanilla ice cream
denada™
sugar free 99.2%
peanut butter ice cream
denada™
denada™
sugar free 98.6%
espresso choc fudge vegan ice cream
no added sugar. all natural 475ml
denada™
sugar free 99.6%
double choc ice cream
no added sugar. all natural 475ml
denada™
sugar free 99.6%
mint chip ice cream
no added sugar. all natural 475ml
denada™
sugar free 98.3%
raspberry ribbon ice cream
no added sugar. all natural

52

Orbita

Requena → andresrequena.es

Orbita Coffee sits within a competitive market, which is why Requena needed to project a strong differential, evocative, brave and unique identity, surpassing the pretentious concepts associated with the specialty coffee industry.

The graphic identity is a direct reference to the name of the brand. It contains a strong symbolic meaning, while at the same time it's abstract and interpretable enough to be used as an expressive, visual trigger.

The brand avoids anything static, helping to comprise a discourse of constant evolution, movement, and change, exactly like the gravitational trajectory of an orbit.

ORBITA
COFFEE
Lanzamiento Espacial
Consell de Cent, 227
OMA
BISTRO
16.09.21
18H
orbita.coffee

ORBITA
orbita coffee 250g

Head roaster
orbita.coffee
Spacealty Coffee
ORBITA
Spacealty Coffee
Spacealty Coffee
ORBITA
rbita.coffee

Jardins de Métis

Principle → principal.studio
This campaign design was for the 22nd edition of the International Garden Festival, which takes place at Jardins de Métis, in Bas-Saint-Laurent.

For the 2021 edition, the most important contemporary garden festival in North America had as its theme 'The magic outside'.

Festival
international
de jardins
26 juin—
3 octobre
2021
Jardins de Métis

al
ational
dins

Hydro Québec
Partenaire depuis 1999

26 juin—
3 octobre
2021
s de Métis
gie est dehors
ition

Jardins de Métis 200, route 132, Grand-Métis, Québec www.jardinsdemetis.com

Festival
internati
de jardin

Jardins d
La magie
22e éditi

Festival international de jardins

26 ju
3 oc
202

Jardins de Mé
La magie est d
22e édition

60

Infinite Love Marathon Concerts

Untitled Macao → untitledmacao.com
The 'Infinite Love Marathon Concerts' were held at the Sai Van Lake Plaza, in Macao. They brought together around 300 local entertainers to give marathon musical performances for a total of 44 hours, over nine consecutive days. Their aim was to provide music to help uplift the soul and infuse vitality into society.

一意一心馬拉松
音樂會
Infinite
Love
Marathon
Concerts
Maratona de
Concertos
Amor
Infinito
2022

IC Art 藝文棧
澳門文化局 IC
一意一心
馬拉松
音樂會
Infinite
Love
Marathon
Concerts
www.icm.gov.mo
2022
02.12-20
澳門特別行政區政府文化局
Maratona de
Concertos
Amor Infinito

一意一心
馬拉松音樂會
Love Infinite
Marathon
Concerts
Maratona de
Concertos
Amor Infinito
2022
02.12–20
www.icm.gov.mo
IC Art 藝文棧
澳門文化局 IC
澳門特別行政區政府文化局
INSTITUTO CULTURAL do Governo da Região Administrativa Especial de Macau

一意一心
馬拉松音樂會
Love Infinite
Marathon
Concerts
www.icm.gov.mo
2022
02.12–20
IC Art 藝文棧
澳門文化局 IC
澳門特別行政區政府文化局
INSTITUTO CULTURAL do Governo da Região Administrativa Especial de Macau

64

Visible Invisible

Fakepaper → fakepaper.fr

'Visible Invisible' was an exhibition that was part of BAP (Biennale d'Architecture et de Paysage), the 2nd edition of an architecture and landscaping biennial based in Versailles in France.

The theme of this exhibition was to question what is visible or not in architectural issues today, like hydraulic or wind energy for example.

Fakepaper decided to develop an identity around the idea of the four elements of life but twisted in a 'pop & acid' version. Each life element is symbolised by a colour: **1.** Fire: orange, **2.** Earth: brown, **3.** Water: blue, **4.** Air: grey. Fakepaper chose to add to them the 'sun' (yellow), the 'greenery' (green) and the 'quintessence' (pink), which is a life and universe element in Greek mythology.

They incorporated them with a large repertoire of more than 60 shapes they designed to create the visual language.

Each biennial contributor was assigned a unique shape created by Fakepaper and a reinterpretation of life's elements (fire, earth, water etc) created from images found on web.

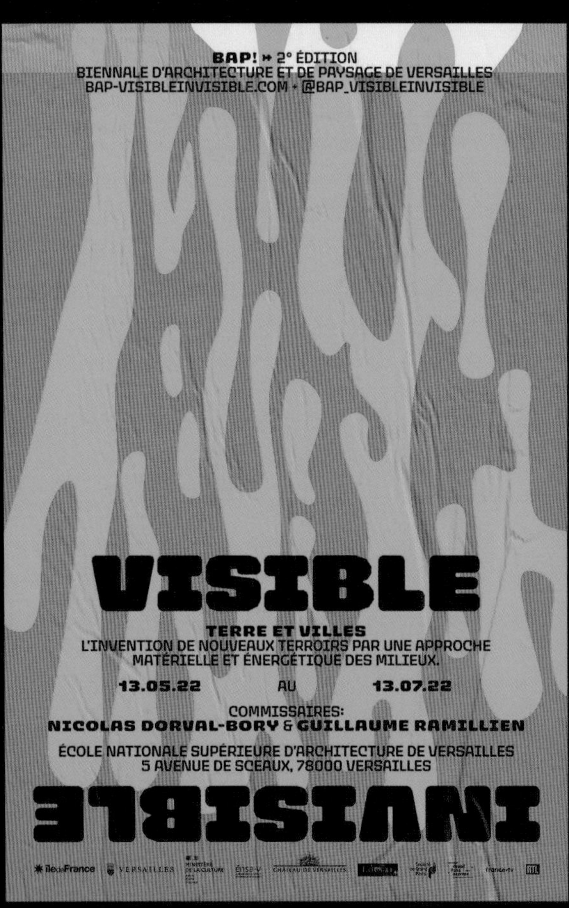

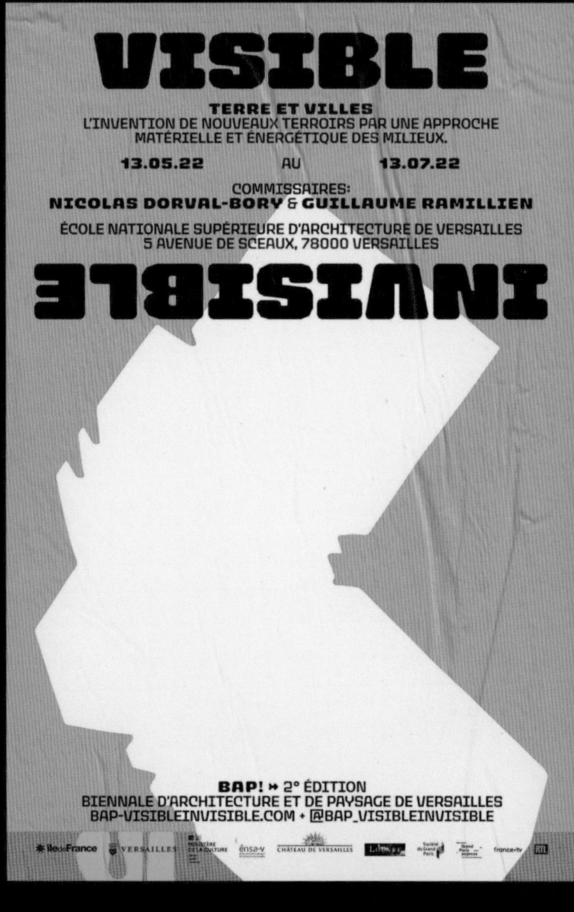

12:10
bap_visibleinvisible
81 Publications
2083 Abonnés
492 Abonnements
Visible, Invisible
Part of @bapidf — 2nd biennale of landscape & architecture
@ensa_versailles exhibition curated by @nicolas_db & @guillaumeramillien plus
www.bap-visibleinvisible.com
Voir la traduction
Suivi par guillaumeramillien, nicolas_db et 7 autres personnes
Abonné(e)
Écrire

12:27
BAP_VISIBLEINVISIBLE
Publications
bap_visibleinvisible
LAURÉATS WORKSHOP
PORTO ACADEMY
Aimé par raphkidd et 49 autres personnes
bap_visibleinvisible @portoacademy visiting

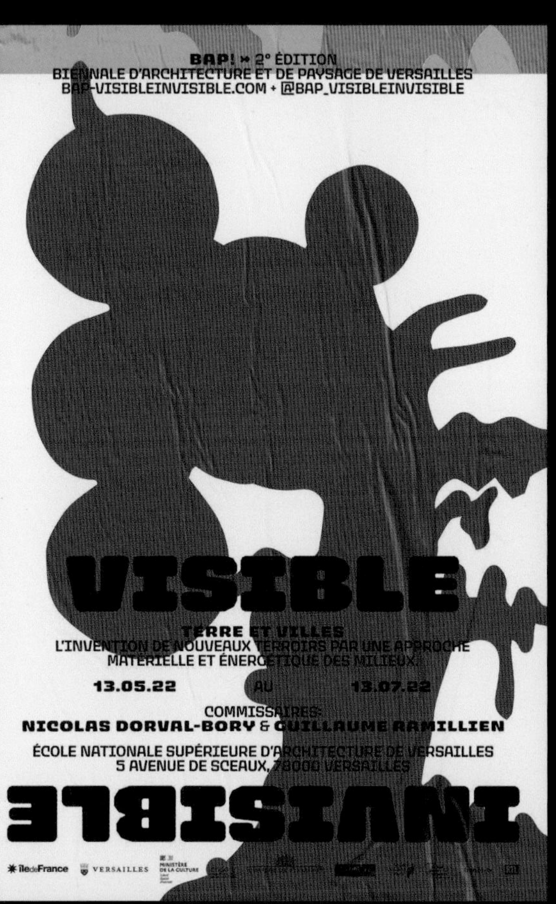
BAP! » 2° ÉDITION
BIENNALE D'ARCHITECTURE ET DE PAYSAGE DE VERSAILLES
BAP-VISIBLEINVISIBLE.COM + @BAP_VISIBLEINVISIBLE
VISIBLE
TERRE ET VILLES
L'INVENTION DE NOUVEAUX TERROIRS PAR UNE APPROCHE
MATÉRIELLE ET ÉNERGÉTIQUE DES MILIEUX.
13.05.22 AU 13.07.22
COMMISSAIRES:
NICOLAS DORVAL-BORY & GUILLAUME RAMILLIEN
ÉCOLE NATIONALE SUPÉRIEURE D'ARCHITECTURE DE VERSAILLES
5 AVENUE DE SCEAUX, 78000 VERSAILLES
INVISIBLE
îledeFrance
VERSAILLES
MINISTÈRE DE LA CULTURE

VISIBLE
TERRE ET VILLES
L'INVENTION DE NOUVEAUX TERROIRS PAR UNE APPROCHE
MATÉRIELLE ET ÉNERGÉTIQUE DES MILIEUX.
13.05.22 AU 13.07.22
COMMISSAIRES:
NICOLAS DORVAL-BORY & GUILLAUME RAMILLIEN
ÉCOLE NATIONALE SUPÉRIEURE D'ARCHITECTURE DE VERSAILLES
5 AVENUE DE SCEAUX, 78000 VERSAILLES
INVISIBLE
BAP! » 2° ÉDITION
BIENNALE D'ARCHITECTURE ET DE PAYSAGE DE VERSAILLES
BAP-VISIBLEINVISIBLE.COM + @BAP_VISIBLEINVISIBLE
îledeFrance
VERSAILLES
MINISTÈRE DE LA CULTURE

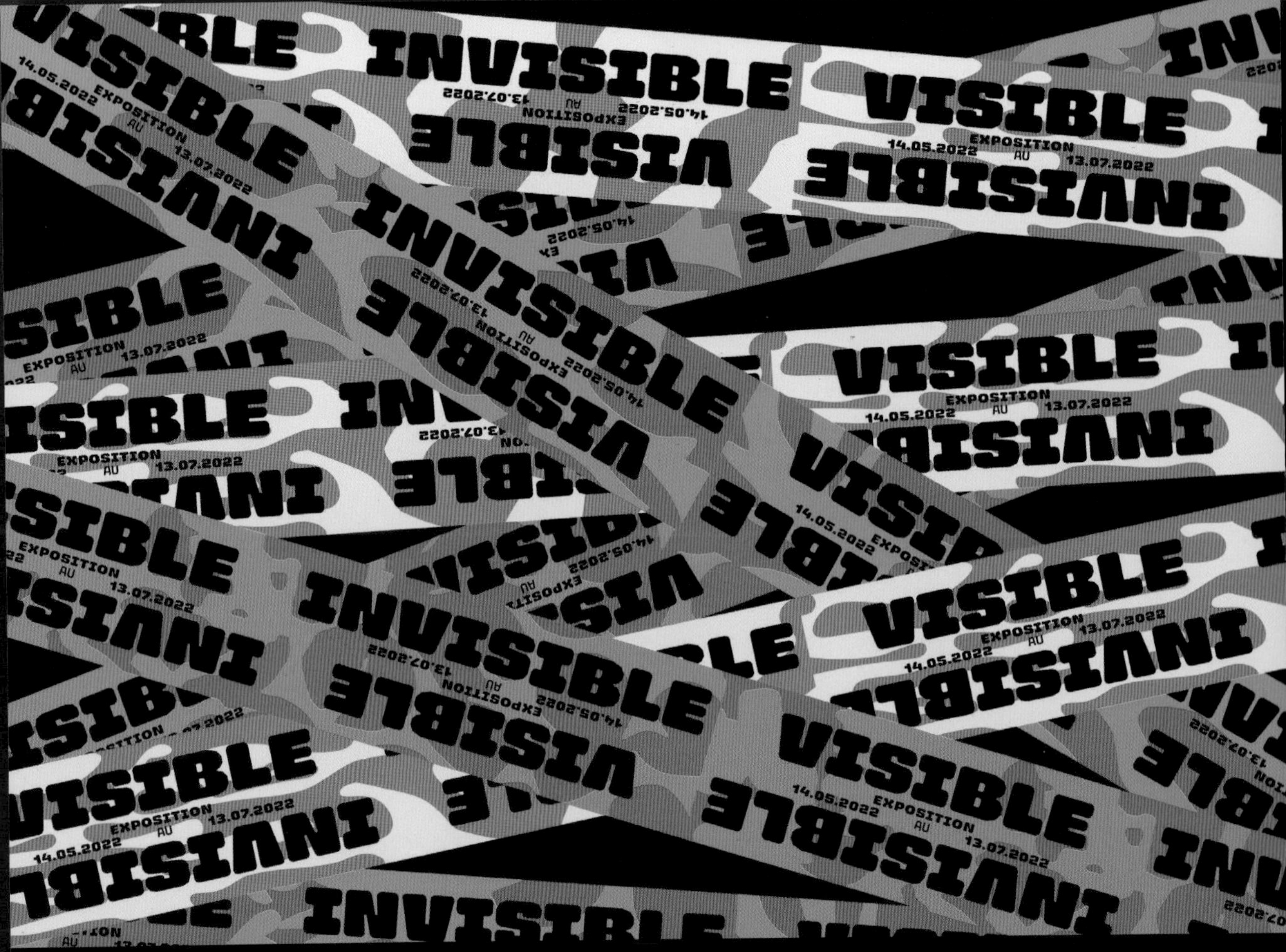

VISIBLE
INVISIBLE
EXPOSITION
14.05.2022 AU 13.07.2022

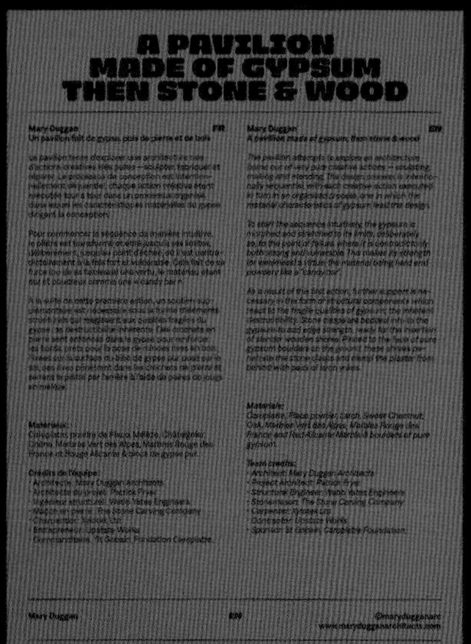

Mary Duggan FR
Un pavillon fait de gypse, puis de pierre et de bois

Mary Duggan EN
A pavilion made of gypsum, then stone & wood

Mary Duggan
@marydugganarc
www.marydugganarchitects.com

INVITÉS INTERNATIONAUX — COUR DES FONTAINES

FR » » EN

BAP ! 2022 » 2E ÉDITION
14.05.2022 AU 13.07.2022

INSTAGRAM » CONTACT »

COMMISSARIAT EXPOSITIONS ÉVÈNEMENTS PRATIQUE

COMMISSAIRES

NICOLAS DORVAL-BORY & GUILLAUME RAMILLIEN

FACE À L'URGENCE ÉCOLOGIQUE DE NOUVELLES ARCHITECTURES SONT EN TRAIN D'ÉMERGER EN ÎLE-DE-FRANCE, SUR TOUT LE TERRITOIRE MAIS AUSSI PARTOUT DANS LE MONDE. POUR LES INVENTER, LEURS AUTEURS S'INTERROGENT SUR CE QUI EST À LA SOURCE DE L'ARCHITECTURE EN DÉVELOPPANT DE NOUVEAUX LANGAGES OSCILLANTS AINSI ENTRE ARCHITECTURE VISIBLE ET INVISIBLE.

« LA CABANE OU LE FEU ? »

SI UN TERROIR PEUT ÊTRE DÉFINI COMME LA RENCONTRE D'UN SOL, D'UN CLIMAT ET DE SAVOIR-FAIRE, L'ARCHITECTURE EST DE FAÇON SIMILAIRE LA MISE EN FORME, AU TRAVERS D'UNE CULTURE PARTICULIÈRE, DE MATIÈRES ET DE CLIMATS INTÉRIEURS, DES RESSOURCES VISIBLES ET INVISIBLES.

EN 1969, LE CRITIQUE REYNER BANHAM DÉFINIT L'ARCHITECTURE COMME UNE STRATÉGIE DOUBLE LIÉE À UN MILIEU, ET L'ILLUSTRE PAR L'HISTOIRE D'UNE TRIBU QUI « ARRIVERAIT AU SOIR DANS UN CAMPEMENT BIEN APPROVISIONNÉ EN BOIS ». POUR SATISFAIRE À SA CONDITION HOMÉOTHERME FACE À LA NUIT, LE POTENTIEL DE CE BOIS PEUT ÊTRE EXPLOITÉ SELON DEUX MÉTHODES : CONSTRUIRE UN ABRI — LA SOLUTION STRUCTURELLE —, OU ALIMENTER UN FEU OU UN FOYER — LA SOLUTION ÉNERGÉTIQUE.

UN DEMI-SIÈCLE PLUS TARD, ET FACE AUX ENJEUX ENVIRONNEMENTAUX, L'EXPOSITION VISIBLE, INVISIBLE INTERROGE LES FORMES ARCHITECTURALES CONTEMPORAINES QUI PEUVENT NAÎTRE DE CETTE REDÉCOUVERTE DE LA RATIONALITÉ MATÉRIELLE ET ÉNERGÉTIQUE.

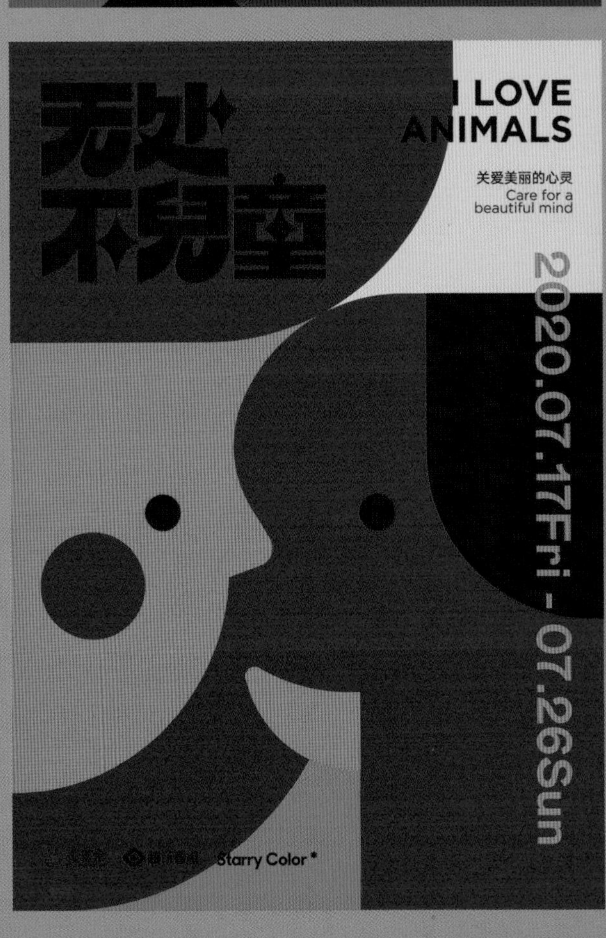

Everywhere There Are Kids

Cheng Peng → behance.net/kabaopeng

For this exhibition for autistic children, Cheng Peng made a series of posters on the theme of 'Caring for Beautiful Minds'.

Autistic children are just as curious about the world as any other children. Noting that they often love animals, plants, sunshine and rain, Cheng Peng's hope was that these posters would, 'attract attention with simple graphics and bright colour combinations and call on society to understand their beautiful minds, without labels'.

I LOVE STARS

关爱美丽的心灵

Care for a beautiful mind

壹基金 One Foundation

腾讯看点

Starry Color*

2020.07.17Fri - 07.27Sun

无处不見童

无处
不兒童

I LOVE
SPRING

关爱美丽的心灵
Care for a
beautiful mind

2020.07.17Fri - 07.26Sun

Starry Color *

腾讯看点

Starry Color *

I LOVE FRUIT

关爱美丽的心灵

Care for a beautiful mind

2020.07.17 Fri - 07.26 Sun

无处
不兒童

2021
HAPPY NEW YEAR
ANNÉE DU BOEUF
BONNE ANNÉE

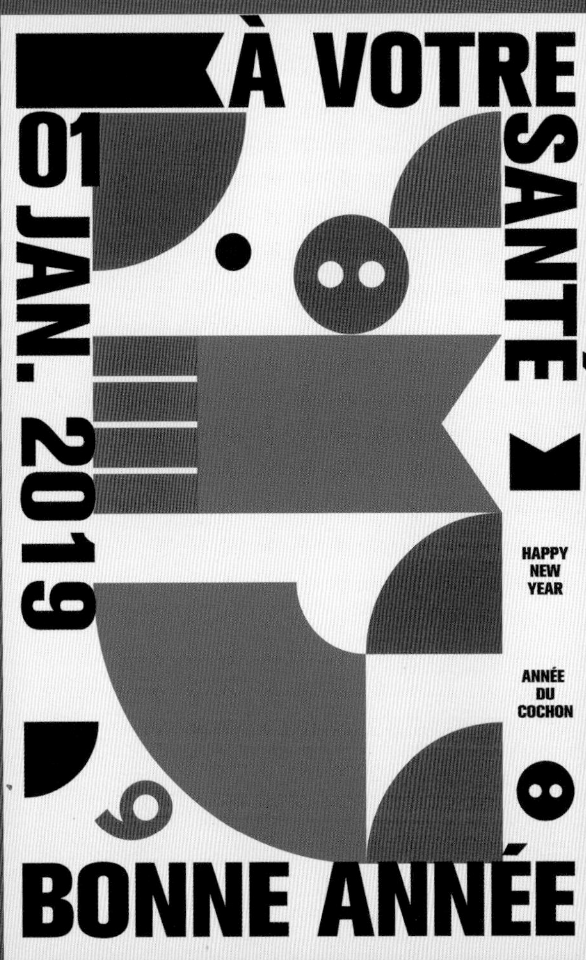

Chinese Zodiac Series Poster 1

Cheng Peng → behance.net/kabaopeng
Inspired by the Chinese zodiac, Cheng Peng created a series of posters using six of its animals: the pig, the mouse, the snake, the ox, the tiger and the monkey, trying to represent the characteristics of these animals with simple geometric shapes and colours. Cheng Peng's hope is that people will have fresh feelings about Chinese traditions through her works.

01 JAN. 2028

BON APPÉTIT

HAPPY
NEW
YEAR

ANNÉE
DU
SINGE

BONNE ANNÉE

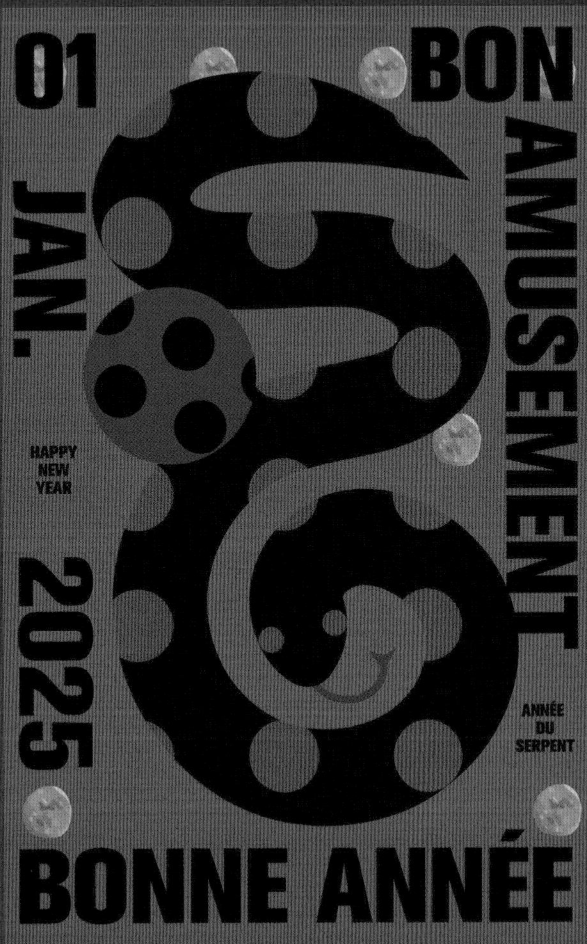

'Inspired by the Chinese zodiac, Cheng Peng created a series of posters using six of its animals.'

Benshi

Onion Design → oniondesign.com.tw
Benshi is a publication from the National Kaohsiung Center for the Arts.

The venue is defined as an 'art center for everyone' and the content and form of the publication is meant to be easily read.

The themes of each issue are drawn from daily life, with issues such as: humour, tools, superstition, communication, sound, paper, pictures, sequences, travel and food, etc. It advocates that art is not only esoteric ideas and metaphysical discussions. Everyone can get close to art, participate in art and live artistic lives.

FEBRUARY
5
本事
工具美

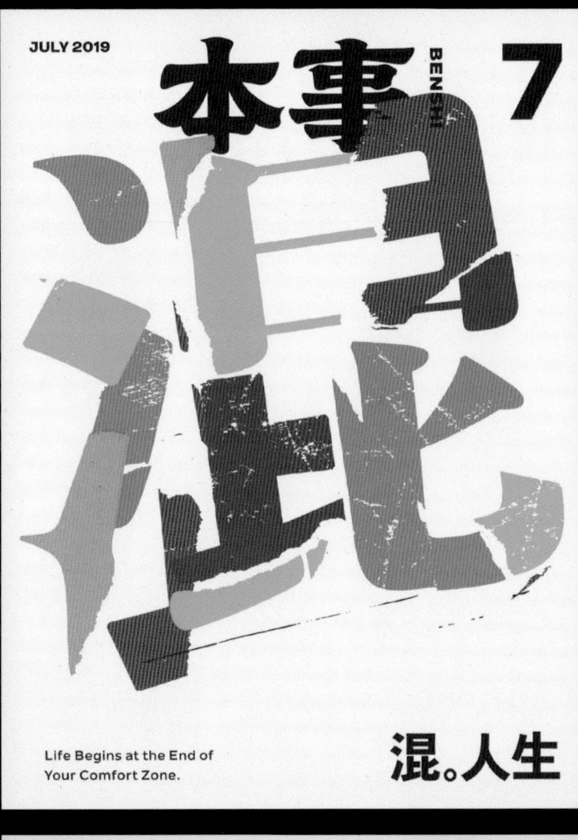
JULY 2019
本事
BENSHI
7
混
Life Begins at the End of
Your Comfort Zone.
混。人生

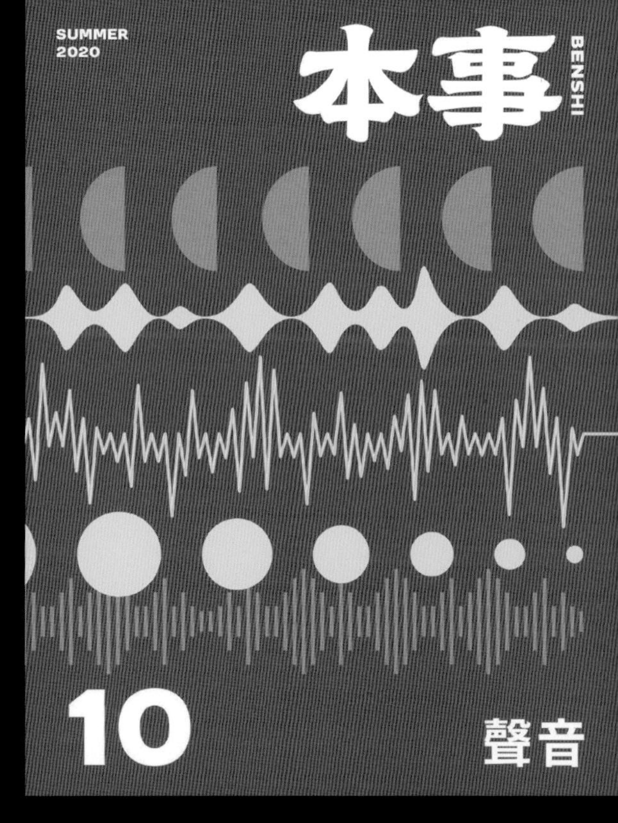
SUMMER
2020
本事
BENSHI
10
聲音

AUTUMN
2020
紙
本
事
BENSHI
11

BENSHI

本事 16

數字衛武營
Numerical Weiwuying (1)

劇場
Theater (5)

京劇
Peking Opera (2)

古典樂
Classical Music (14)

觀劇禮儀
Theater Etiquette (4)

芭蕾
Ballet (2)

打擊樂
Percussion (4)

舞台劇
Drama (7)

聲樂
Vocal Music (11)

指揮
Conductor (4)

實驗音樂
Experimental Music (4)

打開黑盒子
Behind the Stage (14)

現代舞
Modern Dance (6)

你問我答
FAQ (5)

馬戲
Circus (5)

歌劇
Opera (4)

表藝空間
Performance Space (4)

偶戲
Puppet Theater (5)

表演藝術101

Performing Arts 101

Bennetts

Seachange → seachange.studio
Bennetts of Mangawhai are passionate about creating the most exquisite hand-crafted chocolates in New Zealand and have been doing so since 1998. For Easter, Bennetts decided to up their game and challenged Seachange to create a packaging range that was fun and premium in equal measure.

A continuous crack and looping rabbit burrow pattern were created to wrap the golden egg and luxury bunny range. The use of bold, playful colours, and unexpected combinations brought the packaging to life and allowed them to stand out in busy retail spaces. Using colours in a reductive way allowed the range to maintain its sense of quality and premiumness.

'The use of bold, playful colours, and unexpected combinations brought the packaging to life.'

DARK CHOCOLATE
GOLDEN EGG
WITH SEA SALT BUTTONS
Bennetts
MILK CHOCOLATE
GOLDEN EGG
WITH SEA SALT BUTTONS

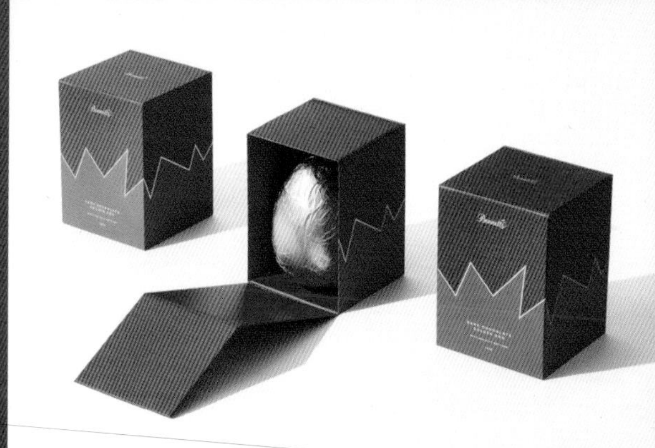

Bennetts
Bennetts
Bennetts
Bennetts
Bennetts

MILK
CHOCOLATE
SQUARES

Bennetts

DARK
CHOCOLATE
SQUARES
Bennetts

MILK
CHOCOLATE
SQUARES
Bennetts

DARK
CHOCOLATE
SQUARES
Bennetts

MILK
CHOCOLATE
SQUARES

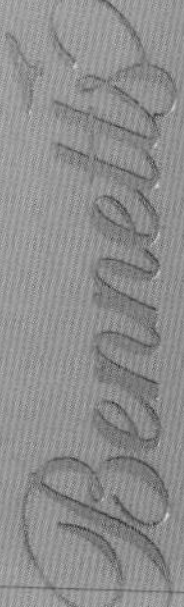
Bennetts

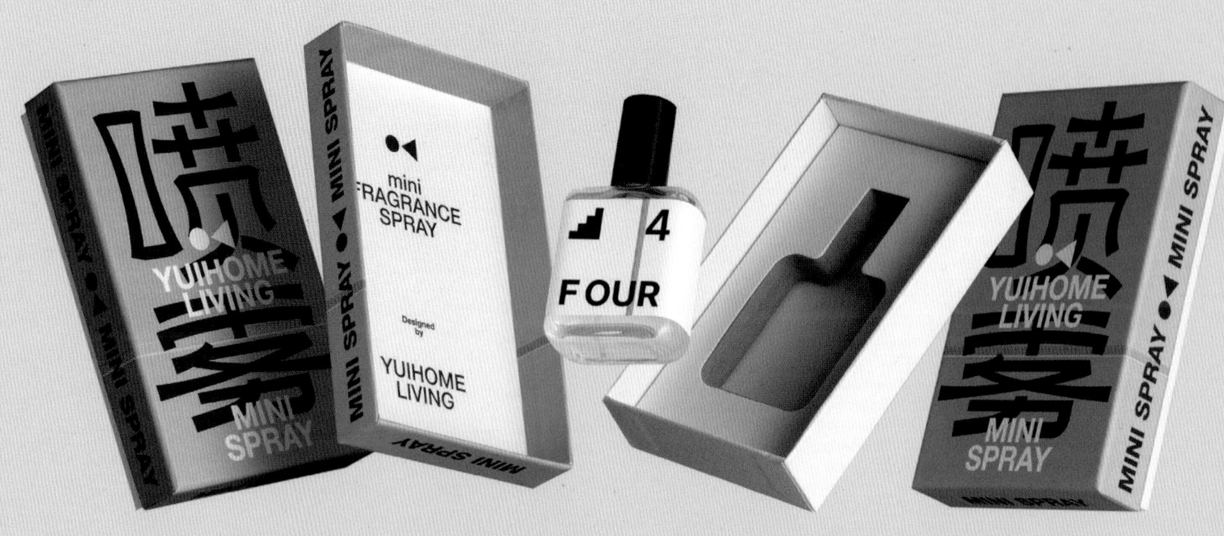

MINISPRAY Package Design

Simin Xu → behance.net/siminxbs

The blue of the outer packaging for this fragrance spray, titled 'Daily Uncountable', is one of the exclusive colours of the 寓义 to Define brand and a variety of auxiliary colours also have been utilised.

The triangles and circles within the design are representations of spray patterns. In the design, the number and scent name are placed on both sides of the bottle, which creates a sense of surprise for the user.

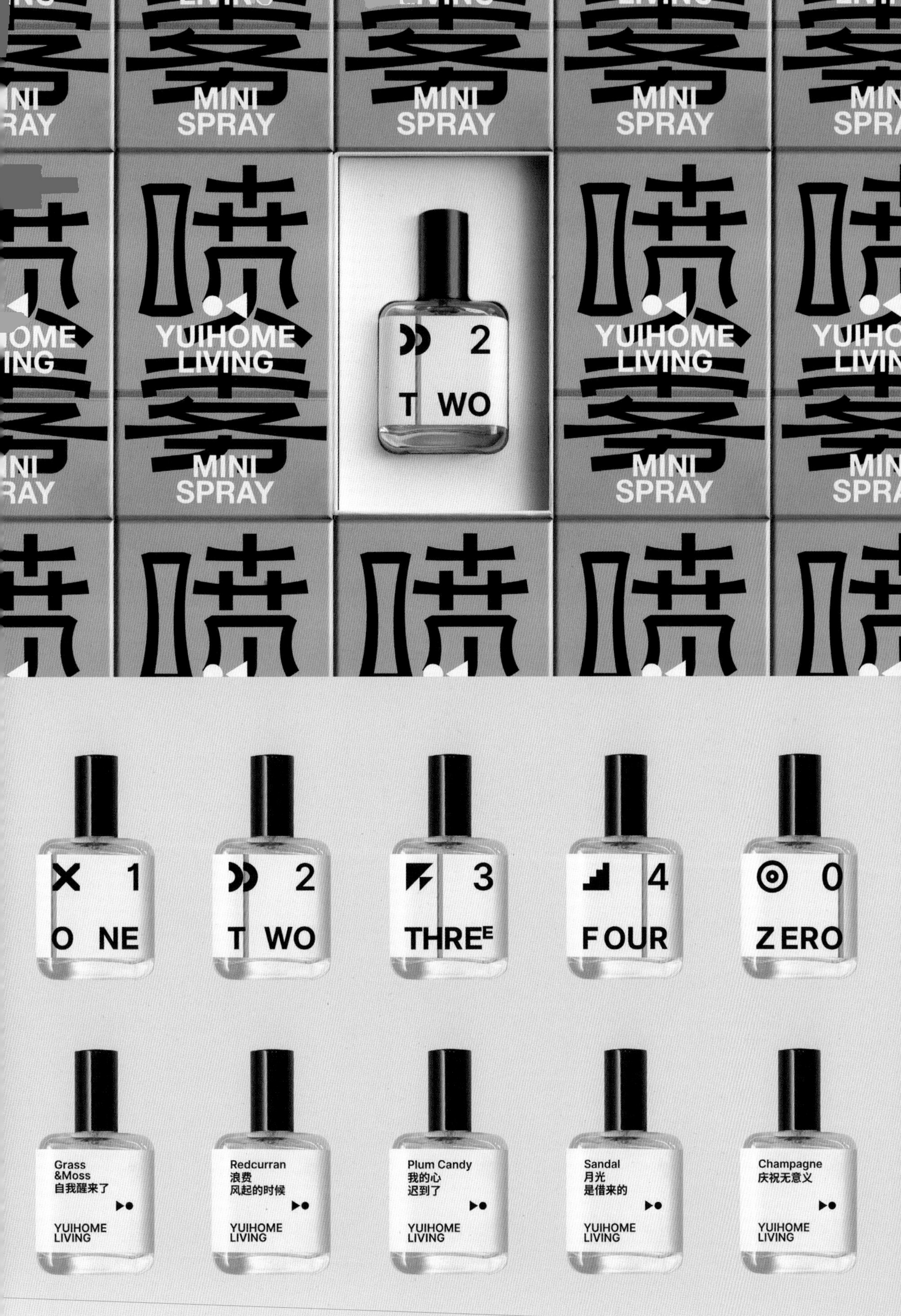
MINI
SPRAY
YUIHOME
LIVING
2
TWO
1
ONE
2
TWO
3
THREE
4
FOUR
0
ZERO
Grass
&Moss
自我醒来了
YUIHOME
LIVING
Redcurran
浪费
风起的时候
YUIHOME
LIVING
Plum Candy
我的心
迟到了
YUIHOME
LIVING
Sandal
月光
是借来的
YUIHOME
LIVING
Champagne
庆祝无意义
YUIHOME
LIVING

Sound of Sunrise

Third Paragraph → thirdparagraph.co

'Sound of Sunrise' was a pop-up exhibition for a book launch of two books from a small Hong Kong publisher. The different tones of gradient depict the colour of sunrise that echoes the stories in the two books.

The reader could engage with the authors at the pop-up event and the exhibition posters shown here could also be used as wrapping paper for the reader to bring the books home in.

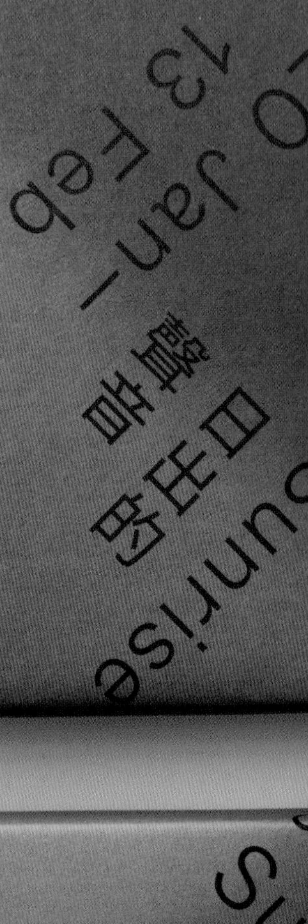

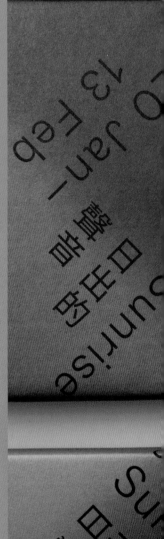

of
Sunrise
日出的
聲音
20 Jan–
13 Feb
StoryTeller
Presents

貓要求他、指令他，他不但不會生氣，還有點樂在其中。
StoryTeller Presents:
Sound of Sunrise
日出的聲音
20 Jan–13 Feb
WeWork New Street Gallery
Sheung Wan
上環
太平山新街13A號
www.storyteller.com.hk @everyone.is.storyteller
Pop-up Book Store & Exhibitions

Sound
of
Sunrise
日出的
聲音
20 Jan—
13 Feb

Perniclas Bedow

Interview 02

Bedow is a design and branding studio based in Stockholm. With rationality, craft and ingenuity they build design solutions for innovators, artists and organisations. The results are progressive, engaging and enduring.

→ bedow.se

'We are very rational when it comes to picking colours, they have to communicate the design narrative or have a clear function.'

What is your background and how did you become involved in graphic design?

After high school, in the mid 90's, I started working at Nintendo in Sweden. I am not a gamer, it was just a coincidence since Nintendo had their headquarters in the city I grew up in. One day they asked me if I could help out with updating their website and they put me on a two day course in HTML and Photoshop. I was 19 and that was my first encounter with graphic design. I didn't realise that I was working with design, but I was hooked immediately. The preciseness and accuracy that came with design was something I had by nature. Every day after work I went home and scanned and edited photographs in Photoshop and designed glyphs in Fontographer. That eventually led me into advertising and in the late 90's I started working as a designer in an advertising agency. In 2005 I started design studio Bedow and today we're eight employees.

What is your studio driven by creatively?

I think the word creativity is a bit overused in our industry and I would like to define the word before answering the question: to me creativity is to solve a defined problem in an unexpected way. Sometime, somewhere, someone in our industry took ownership of that word and today it seems to be a truth that we, designers, are more creative than other professions. We owe that person a lot, since we're the ones capitalising on it now. But I don't believe that designers are more creative, I believe that all humans can solve problems in unexpected ways, just within different contexts. You just need to find your method of solving problems and nurture it. So to answer the question, for us writing is a good tool. Design is a very abstract task and being able to formulate what to do before you do it is crucial for us. We're the opposite of intuition, we're the mother of rationality.

How important is colour to your work?

I have never seen us as a colourful design studio and I have never seen colour as an important tool in our work. Colours can be interpreted in so many ways and is not much of a communication tool, it's mainly decoration to me and something we add at the end of our process. We often use colour for functional purposes – for communicative purposes I prefer to use one or two colours only. Sometimes, if the client is eager to have a colourful brand, we add more colours. But it's not so often it turns out better with more.

Do you have a favourite colour?

I like all colours, it's just that they belong in different contexts. If I am in the forest I think green is a nice colour to wear, to blend in. If I am skiing I think a contrasting colour is nice, to not blend in. With that said, it doesn't mean that I don't like colours – it can be fantastic, and I envy designers who create colourful work that is just beautiful – it's just that I have always struggled with incorporating colours into our work. They have to be there for a reason, not just decoration. I am working on a poster for a client right now and it will probably sell better if it's colourful, so I am trying to incorporate some.

How do you stop your personal preferences getting in the way of what is required for the client?

We are very rational when it comes to picking colours, they have to communicate the design narrative or have a clear function.

How important is harmony within your colour palettes? Is it always necessary?

It is important and probably also the hardest thing. That is maybe the reason why we try to use as few colours as possible. Mo colours, mo problems or what was it that Biggie was rapping about?

How can an effective colour palette enhance a brand's identity?

To the untrained eye, colour is the first thing to appreciate. I showed the poster mentioned above to my ten year old son the other day and he said, 'I like the colours, Dad'. Colour is a very basic tool for a designer, so I would say that an appropriate colour palette can be a very effective door opener to a brand. It's like the smell of new baked bread when entering someone's home.

Swee Kombucha

Bedow → bedow.se

Swee is a kombucha born in the Georgian capital of Tbilisi, a city with a rich culinary and cultural heritage in its own right, deepened by a myriad of different influences over the centuries. Swee brews its probiotic ferments from a careful selection of local, all-natural ingredients to create a range of refreshing drinks that are delicious and good for the gut.

The brand identity is built around the tagline '100% natural', to reflect the brand's commitment to using all-natural ingredients. Visually, this is communicated through two different modular systems, one of which focuses on the drink's unique list of ingredients and the other on the symbiotic nature of the drink itself; a word mark which comes in 10 different iterations and represents the bacteria and yeast from which a kombucha SCOBY is formed.

Swee's ingredient list forms the basis of its identity, taking what is typically functional information and turning it into a visually rich infographic system. Each ingredient is represented by a bespoke colour and pattern which combine to create unique chromatic graphics, representing the percentage value of each ingredient. This offers limitless potential for variation as the brand grows its offering and clearly embodies the brand's tagline.

'Each ingredient is represented by a bespoke colour and pattern which combine to create unique chromatic graphics, representing the percentage value of each ingredient.'

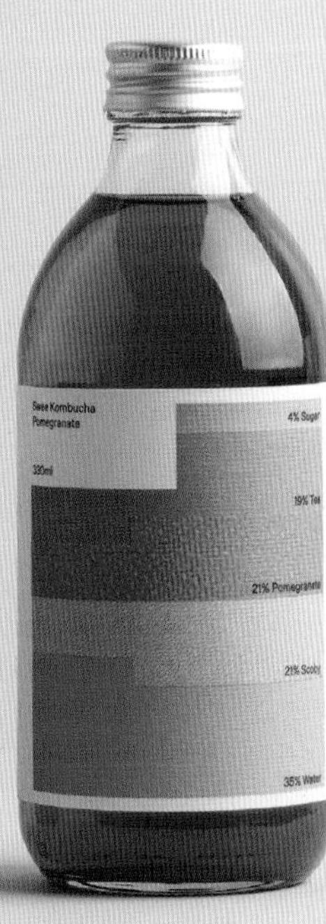

35% Water
21% Scoby
Swee Kombucha

20% Feijoa
16% Tea
5% Sugar
3% Ginger
100% Natural

Blissful of Eid Al Fitr

Nero Atelier → nero-graphic.com

Indonesia is a country with the largest Muslim population in the world. It is not surprising that the celebration of Eid is always eagerly awaited every year.

To celebrate Eid al-Fitr, Nero Atelier distributied exclusive hampers for relatives and partners. This year's theme was 'Blissful of Eid Al Fitr'.

By combining modern design with local content, Nero Atelier hoped to create a unique, epic and exclusive hamper.

Creative Director & Designer: Yohanes Raymond

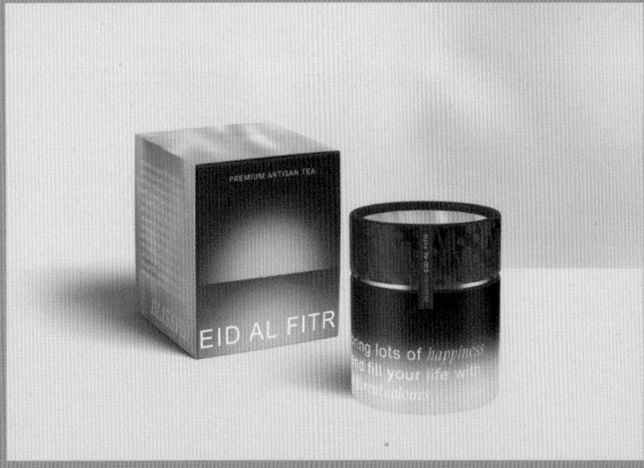

EID AL FITR
BLISSFUL
PREMIUM ARTISAN TEA
Indonesia is one of the best tea producing countries in the world, and that is the reason for us to launch an exclusive Lebaran
- Artisan Tea for our relatives
partnership. And all of them
designed in an epic way,
combining two modern elements
and local content, which can
introduce tea and Indonesian
culture to the international world
through the packaging design of
artisan tea - Blissfull of Eid Al Fitr

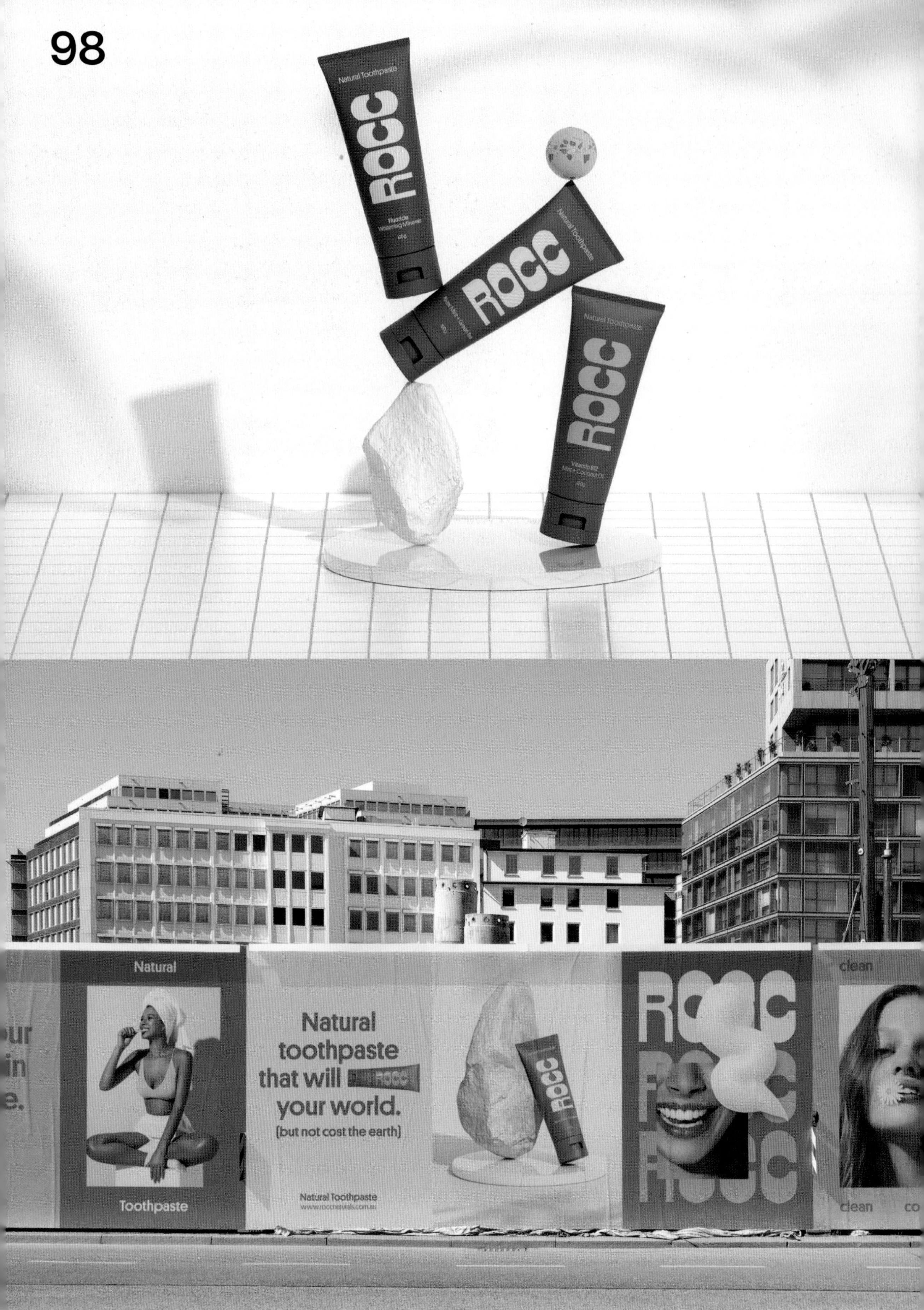
Natural Toothpaste
ROCC
Fluoride
Whitening Minerals
Natural Toothpaste
ROCC
Natural Toothpaste
ROCC
Vitamin B12
Mint + Coconut Oil
Natural
Toothpaste
Natural
toothpaste
that will ROCC
your world.
[but not cost the earth]
Natural Toothpaste
www.roccnaturals.com.au
ROCC
clean
clean

ROCC

Date of Birth → dateofbirth.com.au

ROCC is unique from other natural toothpastes out there in the market in that it thinks about footprints almost as much as teeth.

Date of Birth were tired of seeing the same 'natural' recycled look on other brands, and created a visual identity that looked both nostalgic and brand new at the same time. Something you would love to have sit proudly on your sink, not in your drawer.

(Naturally)
Whiter Teeth
Naturally Derived
Ingredients
Cruelty-Free
Certified
Vegan Certified
Biodegradable
Tube
Sustainable
No SLS
No Parabens
No Triclosan
No Diethanolamine (DEA)
No Aspartame
No Titanium Dioxide
Learn more about our toothpaste at
roccnaturals.com.au
B12 Mint +
Coconut Oil
ROCC
Natural Toothpaste
Vitamin B12
Mint + Coconut Oil
100g
Who doesn't want
to be connected?
@roccnaturals
Rocc Naturals was founded with a drive to things differently: to do better.
Co-Founder Prue Rocchi loves health and fitness. Yoga, half marathons, triathlons... she's tried it all – although not always at a record-breaking pace.
But looking at toothpaste, Prue saw a problem. If we were getting more conscious about how we fuel our body, why were we so relaxed about the ingredients we brush our teeth with?
Prue couldn't find a product that supported her families' oral hygiene and made the world more sustainable. So, she set out to create her own.
One that was:
✓ Natural
✓ Good for the Earth
✓ Formulated to nourish
✓ Designed to sit proudly on the bathroom sink

Cliffor
No stopping
ROCC
roccnaturals.com.au
@roccnaturals
CONTACTLESS PAYMENTS
ON OUR BUSES

TD
JCDecaux
Natural Toothpaste
ROCC
ROCC
Natural Toothpaste
River Mint + Green Tea
100g
ROCC
roccnaturals.com.au
@roccnaturals
168

102

Santo Cielo

Pràctica → practica.design

This visual identity and packaging line was designed for Santo Cielo, a Chinese delicatessen brand that imports traditional Spanish products into China. The project aims to celebrate Spain's culture by capturing the vibranc y of its character.

'¡Santo Cielo!' (similar to Oh My God! in English) is a Spanish expression used to show astonishment when something amazes us. The symbol is made out of exclamation marks to play with this idea, representing a holy halo.

Coming from the nature of the naming, the packaging system is made out of two parts, one reserved to the sacred use of the brand, and the other used to reinforce the Spanish character, through the diverse use of typefaces and colours.

JAMÓN
DE
BELLOTA
IBÉRICO
Santo Cielo
JAMÓN

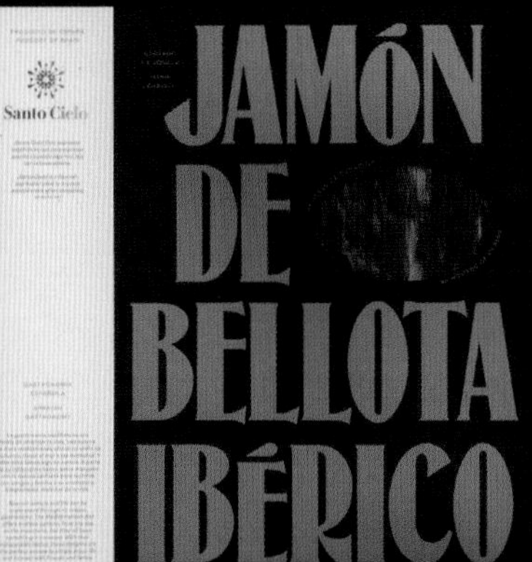
Santo Cielo
JAMÓN
DE
BELLOTA
IBÉRICO

Santo Cielo
JAMÓN
100% NATURAL
SERRANO

Santo Cielo

PRODUCTO DE ESPAÑA
PRODUCT OF SPAIN

Santo Cielo

¡Santo Cielo! Esta expresión española se usa para expresar asombro cuando algo nos deja con la boca abierta.

¡Santo Cielo! is a Spanish expression used to express astonishment when something amazes us!

CORTADO A CUCHILLO
HAND CARVED

JAMÓN

LONCHEADO
SLICED

100%
NATURAL

PRODUCTO DE ESPAÑA
PRODUCT OF SPAIN
Santo Cielo
¡Santo Cielo! Esta expresión española se usa para expresar asombro cuando algo nos deja con la boca abierta.
¡Santo Cielo! is a Spanish expression used to express astonishment when something amazes us!

Santo Cielo

JAMÓN

Santo Cielo
JAMÓN

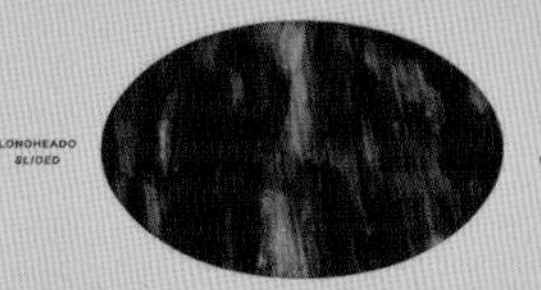
LONCHEADO
SLICED
100%
NATURAL

2021
Art Bank
New Acquisitions
2021
미술은행 신소장품
New
Acquisitions
2021 Art Bank New Acquisitions
미술은행 신소장품
2021 Art Bank New Acquisitions
미술은행 신소장품
2021 Art Bank New Acquisitions
미술은행 신소장품

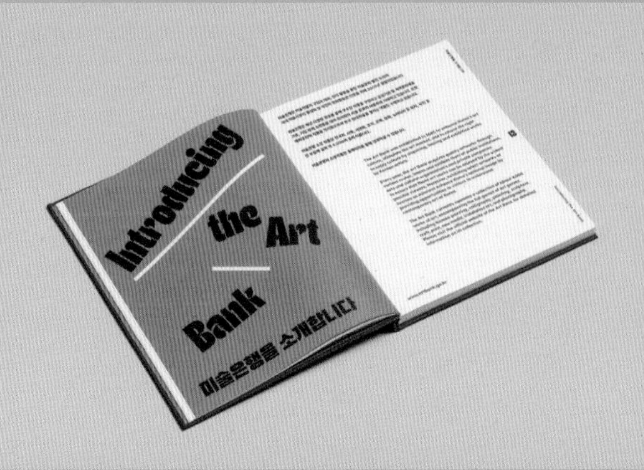

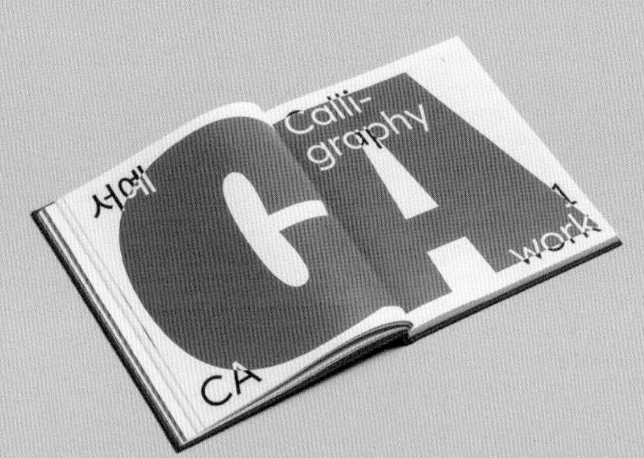

2021 Art Bank New Acquisitions

Everyday Practice → everyday-practice.com
This publication design, by Everyday Practice, was for the 2021 Art Bank New Acquisitions.

The art bank was launched to systematically manage and utilise the collection of the National Museum of Modern and Contemporary Art. Every year, they purchase artworks from various fields and lend them to public institutions and companies to support the spread of art.

Everyday Practice designed and produced catalogues and packages using various physical properties to visualise the nature of art banks that collect and rent art works in various fields such as paintings, sculptures, photographs and media.

Chief Designer: Kwon Joonho
Designer: Kim Juae, Jeon Haeun
Korean Title Lettering: Kim Eojin
Photography: JSK studio

'The poster was designed to hang in each office space, using a bespoke fluorescent ink and printing powered by solar energy.'

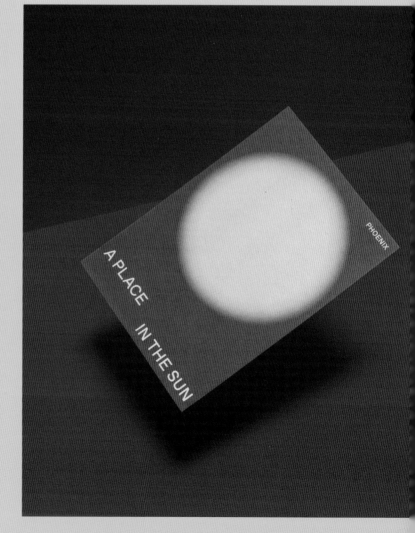

109 Global AR

Eighth Day → eighthday.co.uk

In this identity for Global AR, the bold simplicity of the filled-in 'O', becomes an instantly recognisable global icon, providing plenty of opportunities for engaging applications. This is a logo that is never static, always adapting to the progressive projects it is applied to.

The poster was designed to hang in each office space, using a bespoke fluorescent ink and printing powered by solar energy.

The set of postcards were designed to create a sense of belonging and raise awareness within each team of all Global AR locations. An idiom and fact relating to each location was incorporated, with a message area on the reverse to encourage team members around the globe to communicate with each other.

NEW YORK
TORONTO
A BREATH OF
FRESH AIR
THE WORLD IS
YOUR OYSTER

YORK MINUTE
PHOENIX
A PLACE IN THE SUN
MANILA
FLORIDA
OVER THE MOON

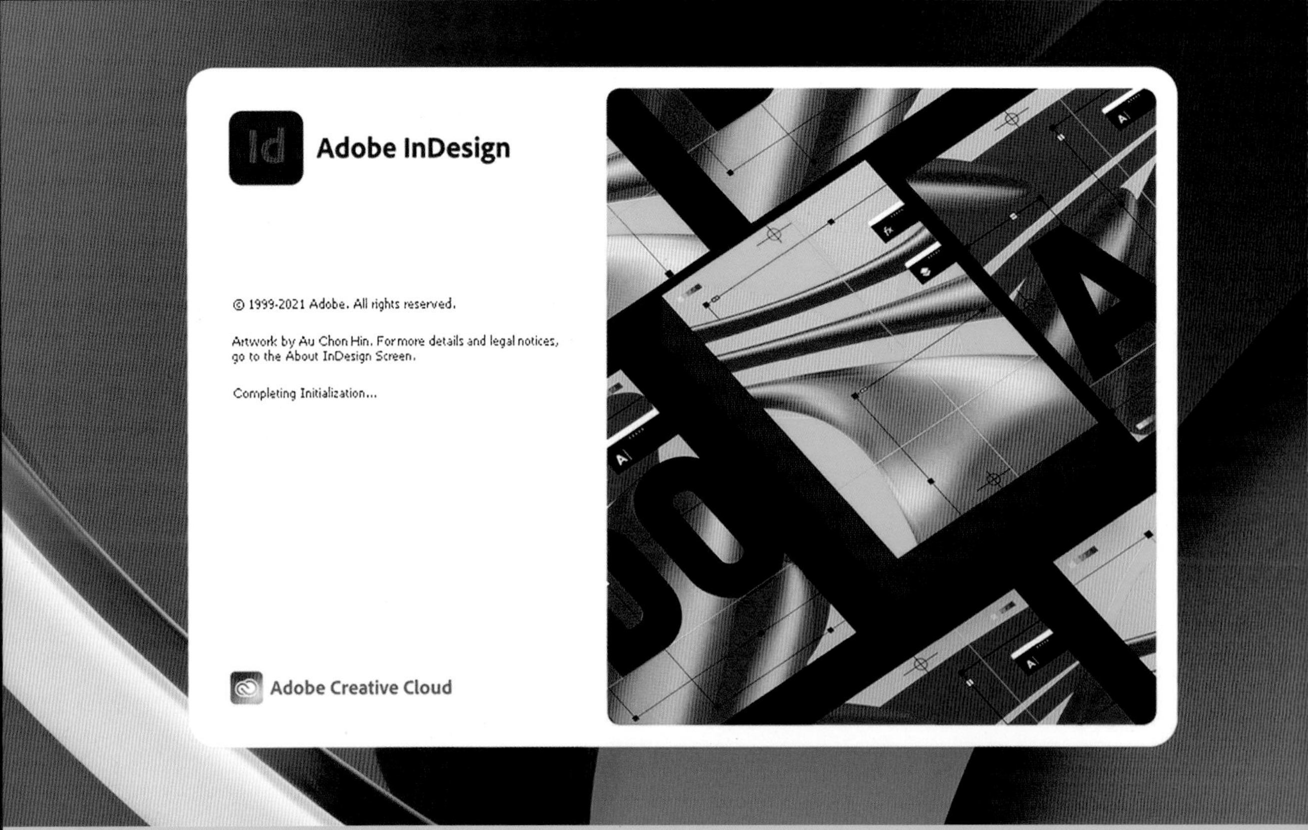

© 1999-2021 Adobe. All rights reserved.

Artwork by Au Chon Hin. For more details and legal notices, go to the About InDesign Screen.

Completing Initialization...

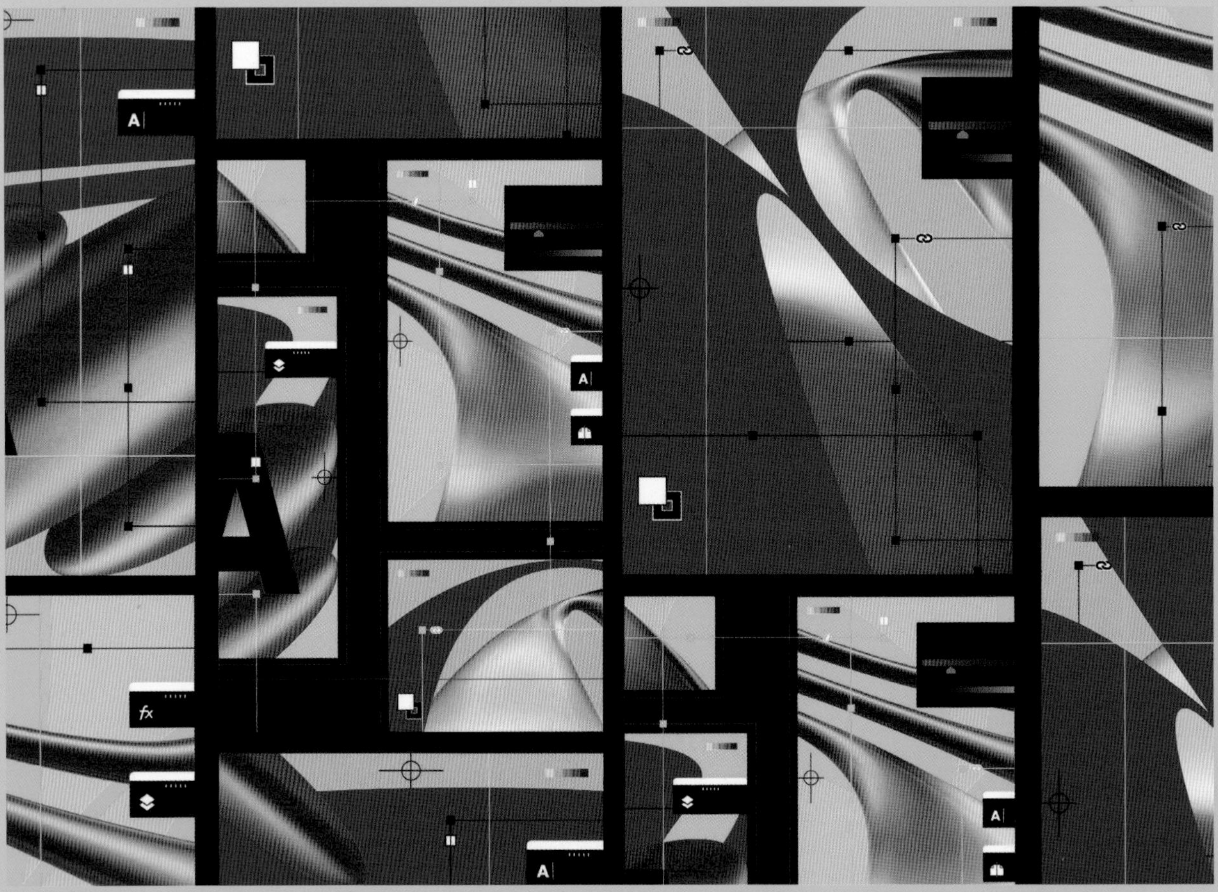

113 Adobe Indesign 2022

Untitled Macao → untitledmacao.com

Untitled Macao chose the theme of 'DNA' for the official image of InDesign. The tools and functions in InDesign represent the DNA of each design work.

With rich imagination, even when they play similar roles, unique visuals can be created and intensified with the creator's own DNA, just like the differences in DNA orders allow everyone to possess qualities and features that are not the same without conflicting.

Visually, a lot of elements are mimicking the functions in Adobe, such as The Tools Panel, Guidelines, etc. They are often seen and used by designers, symbolising the 'DNA' of this software which are intertwined within each single moment of the creative process. As a result, this very design work resonates with every Adobe user.

LowKeyMoves Agency

LEÓN ROMERO → leonromero.work

LowKeyMoves Agency, a creative company working at the intersection of music, culture, content and branding, assigned LEÓN ROMERO to come up with their visual identity and communicative tone of voice. Among the requirements of the brief was the need to implement visual cues that would help distinguish the various types of content they create, while ensuring that the overall identity remained neutral and elegant so as not to overshadow the artists they do work for.

The project was tackled by creating a visual system that would resort to type and a dynamic use of imagery to bring edginess and contrast to the agency's identity. The idea of dynamism and versatility transpired in the formalisation of the agency's logo, which mutates, stretches and compresses according to the medium it's applied to – allowing it to behave like a responsive graphic system. In contrast with the stark typographic treatment, content categories were stylised with a series of circular colour gradients that helped set each type of content apart and make the identity more memorable.

The colourful visual gestures and the type treatment came together to result in an identity that's sober but recognisable; that adapts to various formats and media, without sacrificing its aesthetic appeal or its ability to connect with the audience.

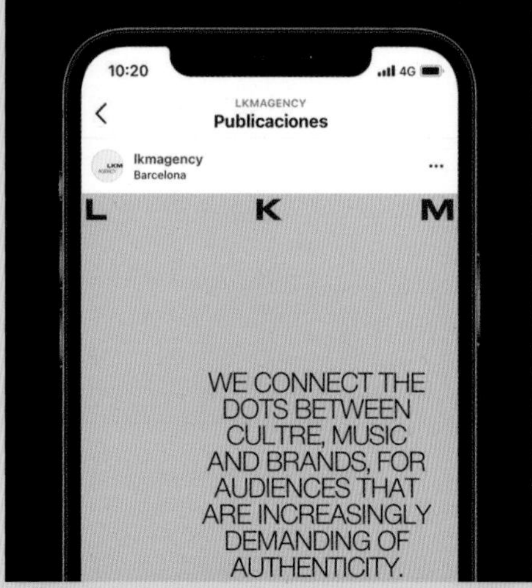

LOWKEYMOVES
MUSIC COMPANY
→ EVNT
@DEPARTAMENTO
ADRIAN BE
AWWZ
DEMMY SOBER
& FRIENDS
LKM
ADRIAN BE
AWWZ
DEMMY SOBER
& FRIENDS
03:00 AM
DEPARTAMENTO
LOWKEYMOVES
LKM
LOWKEYMOVES
MUSIC COMPANY
→ EVNT
BOK BOK
SWEYN J
LADY AMZ
& LOWPROFILE
LKM
11:00 PM
03:00 AM
NIGHT SLUGS
LOWKEYMOVES
LOWKEYMOVES
MUSIC COMPANY
→ EVNT
@ONAC
HIGHKILI
RUMBLER
LA DIABLA
& LE RANSO
LKM
HIGHKILI
RUMBLER
LA DIABLA
LE RANSO
03:00 AM
ONAC
LOWKEYMOVES

LOWKEYMOVES
MUSIC COMPANY

→ EVNT
@LAUT

MANARA
NOAIPRE B2B
COTCH INTL.
LOWPROFILE

27.01.16
11:00 PM → 03:00 AM

MANARA
NOAIPRE B2B
COTCH INTL.
& LOWPROFILE

LKM

27.0
11.00 PM
03:00 AM
COTCH INTL.
LOWKEYMOVES

LOWKEYMOVES
MUSIC COMPANY

→ EVNT
@RAZZMATAZZ

NEANA
BRTSH KNIGHTS
LADY AMZ
& LOWPROFILE

NEANA
BRTSH KNIGHTS
LADY AMZ
LOWPROFILE

LKM

.17

11:00 PM
03:00 AM

COTCH INTL.
LOWKEYMOVES

Mubarak Festival

Nero Atelier → nero-graphic.com
Indonesia has diverse cultures and traditions, however, the majority of Indonesians are Muslims and it has the largest Muslim population in the world.

Nero Atelier participated in Eid Mubarak's celebration with this packaging design inspired by the Indonesian tradition of eating 'ketupat' during Eid Al-Fitr.

Ketupat is a dish made from rice and it is wrapped in young coconut leaves which are woven in a diamond shape. This beautiful and contemporary design was inspired by the formation of the texture and pattern of ketupat.

Creative Director & Designer: Yohanes Raymond

'This beautiful and contemporary design was inspired by the formation of the texture and pattern of ketupat.'

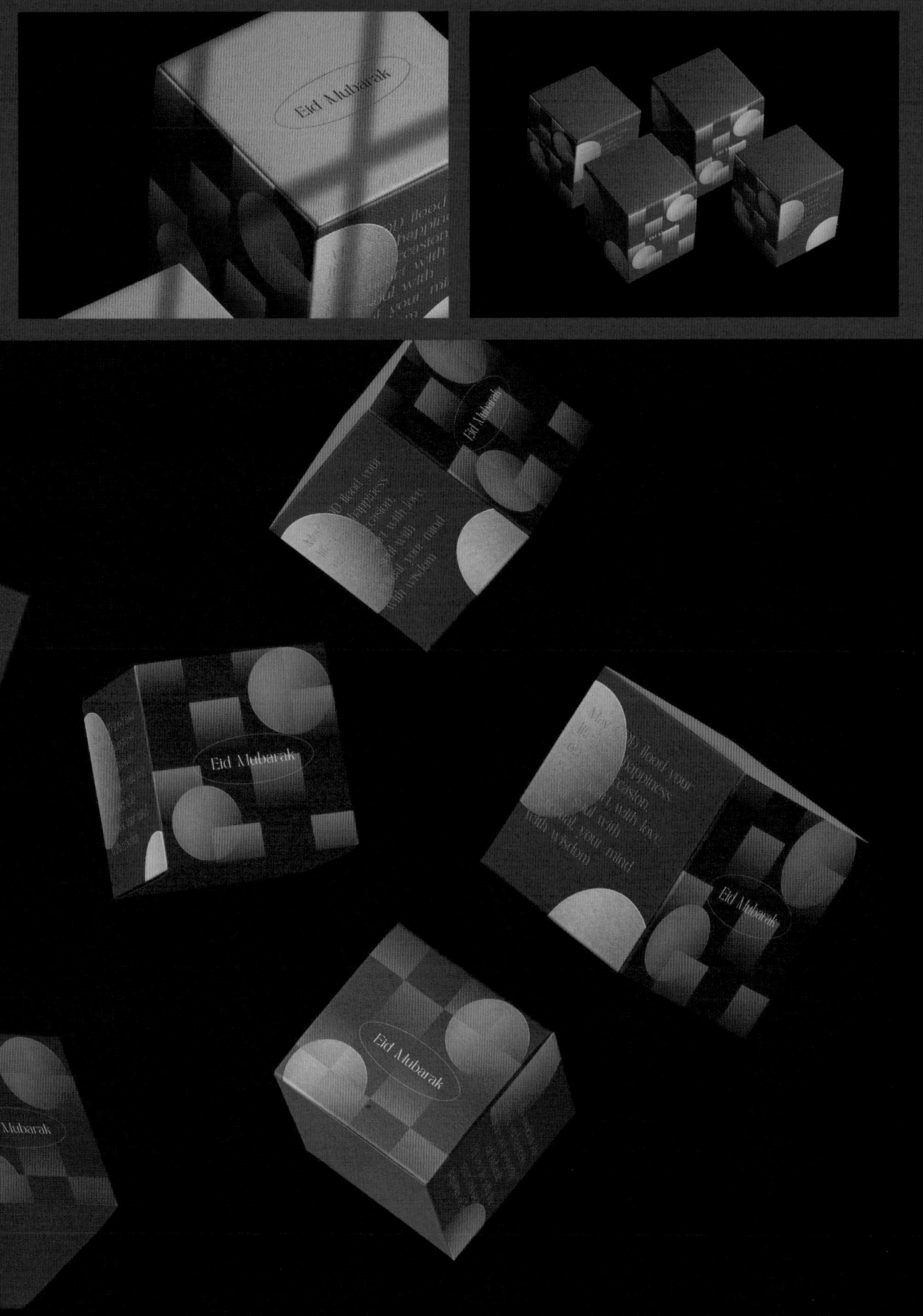
Eid Mubarak
Eid Mubarak
Eid Mubarak
Eid Mubarak
Eid Mubarak
flood your
happiness
with love
your mind
with wisdom

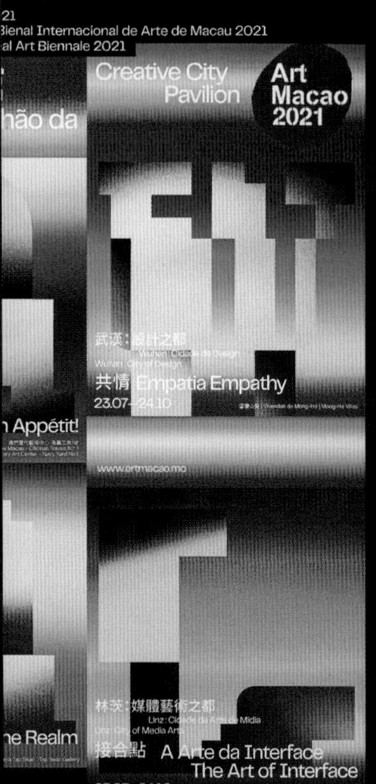
Creative City
Pavilion
Art
Macao
2021
武漢：設計之都
共情 Empatia Empathy
23.07–24.10
www.artmacao.mo
林茨：媒體藝術之都
接合點 A Arte da Interface
The Art of Interface
23.07–24.10

藝文薈澳: 澳門國際藝術雙年展2021
Arte Macau : Bienal Internacional de Arte de Macau 2021
Art Macao : Macao International Art Biennale 2021
創意城市館
Pavilhão da
Cidade Criativa
澳門：美食之都
Macau : Cidade de Gastronomia
Macao : City of Gastronomy
起筷！Bom Apetite! Bon Appétit!
23.07–03.10
南京：文學之都
Nanjing : City of Literature
開境 Abrindo o Reino
Opening Up the Realm
23.07–03.10
Creative City
Pavilion
Art
Macao
2021
武漢：設計之都
共情 Empatia Empathy
23.07–24.10
www.artmacao.mo
林茨：媒體藝術之都
接合點 A Arte da Interface
The Art of Interface
23.07–24.10

藝文薈澳: 澳門國際藝術雙年展2021
Art Macao : Macao International Art Biennale 2021
創意城市館
Pavilhão da
Cidade Criativa
澳門：美食之都
Macau : Cidade de Gastronomia
Macao : City of Gastronomy
起筷！Bom Apetite! Bon Appétit!
23.07–03.10
南京：文學之都
Nanjing : City of Literature
開境 Abrindo o Reino
Opening Up the Realm
23.07–03.10

121

Art Macao 2021 – Creative City Pavilion

Untitled Macao → untitledmacao.com

'Art Macao 2021 – Creative City Pavilion' was committed to creating an immersive cultural atmosphere for the whole city, as a gallery and an art garden.

The 'Creative City Pavilion', which first appeared in 'Art Macao', brings together four UNESCO creative cities, including Macao, the capital of food, Nanjing, the capital of literature, Wuhan, the capital of design, and Linz, the capital of media and art, to connect the world with creativity.

藝文薈澳：澳門國際藝術雙年展2021
Arte Macau : Bienal Internacional de Arte de Macau 2021
林茨：
媒體藝術之都
Linz : Cidade da Arte de Mídia
Linz : City of Media Arts
23.07–24.10
www.artmacao.mo
Art Macao : Macao International Art Biennale 2021
Art Macao 2021
接合點
A Arte da Interface
The Art of Interface
望廈山房
Vivendas de Mong-Há
Mong-Há Villas

藝文薈澳：澳門國際藝術雙年展2021
Arte Macau: Bienal Internacional de Arte de Macau 2021
Art Macao: Macao International Art Biennale 2021
www.artmacao.mo
共情
Empatia
Empathy
Wuhan

藝文薈澳：澳門國際藝術雙年展2021

Arte Macau : Bienal Internacional de Arte de Macau 2021

Art Macao : Macao International Art Biennale 2021

創意城市館

Pavilhão da Cidade Criativa

Creative City Pavilion

Art Macao 2021

南京：文學之都

Nanjing : Cidade da Literatura

Nanjing : City of Literature

www.artmacao.mo

創意城市館總策展人：
Curador Principal :
Chief Curator :

姚風 Yao Feng

策展人：
Curador :
Curator :

黃梵 Huang Fan

參展作家：
Escritores Participantes :
Participating Authors :

蘇童 Su Tong
丁帆 Ding Fan
葉兆言 Ye Zhaoyan
葛亮 Ge Liang
趙本夫 Zhao Benfu
魯敏 Lu Min
韓東 Han Dong
胡弦 Hu Xian
育邦 Yu Bang
馬鈴薯兄弟 Potato Brother
丁捷 Ding Jie
朱輝 Zhu Hui
代薇 Dai Wei
葉輝 Ye Hui
黃小初 Huang Xiaochu
朱贏椿 Zhu Yingchun
少況 Shao Kuang
海波 Hai Bo
孫衍 Sun Yan
丁成 Ding Cheng

(排名不分先後 / por ordem aleatória / in arbitrary order)

開境

Abrindo o Reino

Opening Up the Realm

23.07— 03.10.2021

10:00-19:00

塔石藝文館 | Galeria Tap Seac | Tap Seac Gallery

ArtMacao　IC Art 藝文棧　澳門文化局IC

Secretaria para os Assuntos Sociais e Cultura do Governo da Região Administrativa Especial de Macau

Secretaria para a Economia e Finanças do Governo da Região Administrativa Especial de Macau

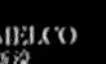

Blanc!

Pràctica → practica.design

This identity was for Blanc!'s 12th edition. Blanc! is a festival that fosters design culture with a very festive approach. This edition's identity was inspired by children's construction games, embracing the festival's didactic goals.

The 'BLANC!' characters are made out of several modules that interact with the festival content, creating a flexible typographic language. Through the chromatic and typographic diversity, Pràctica conveyed the festival's joyful spirit.

Moreover, this 2020 edition was 100% online, therefore all the applications were digital; From social media assets to the audiovisual transmissions (streamings) of the event.

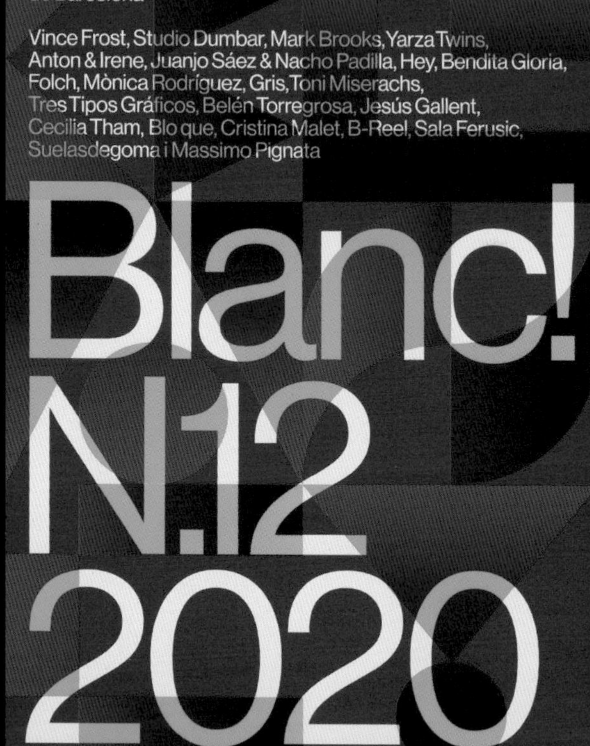

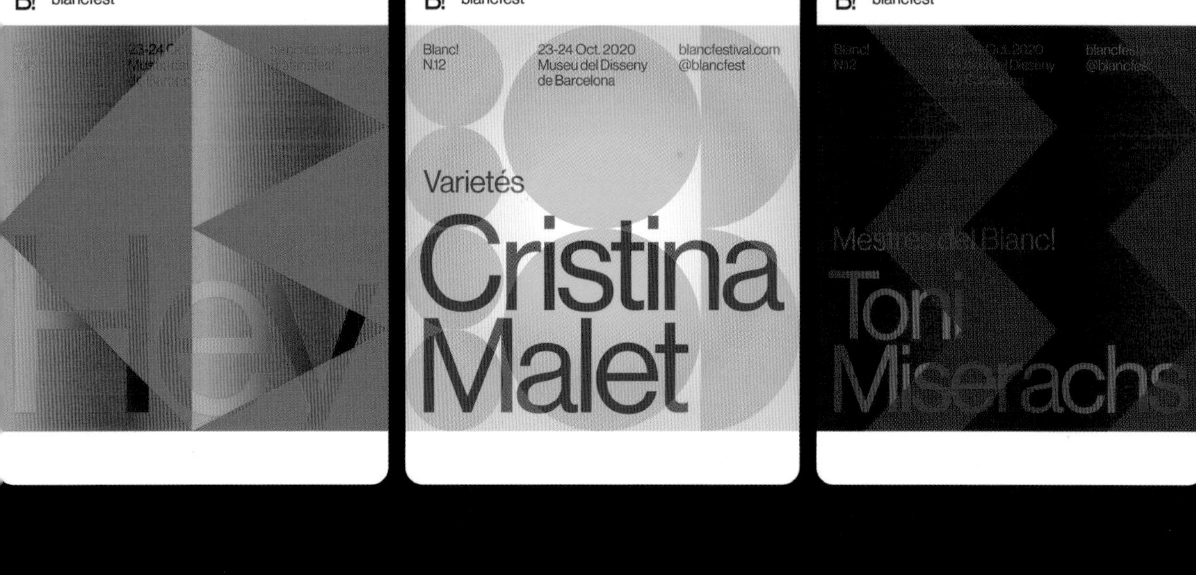

'Through the chromatic and typographic diversity, Pràctica conveyed the festival's joyful spirit.'

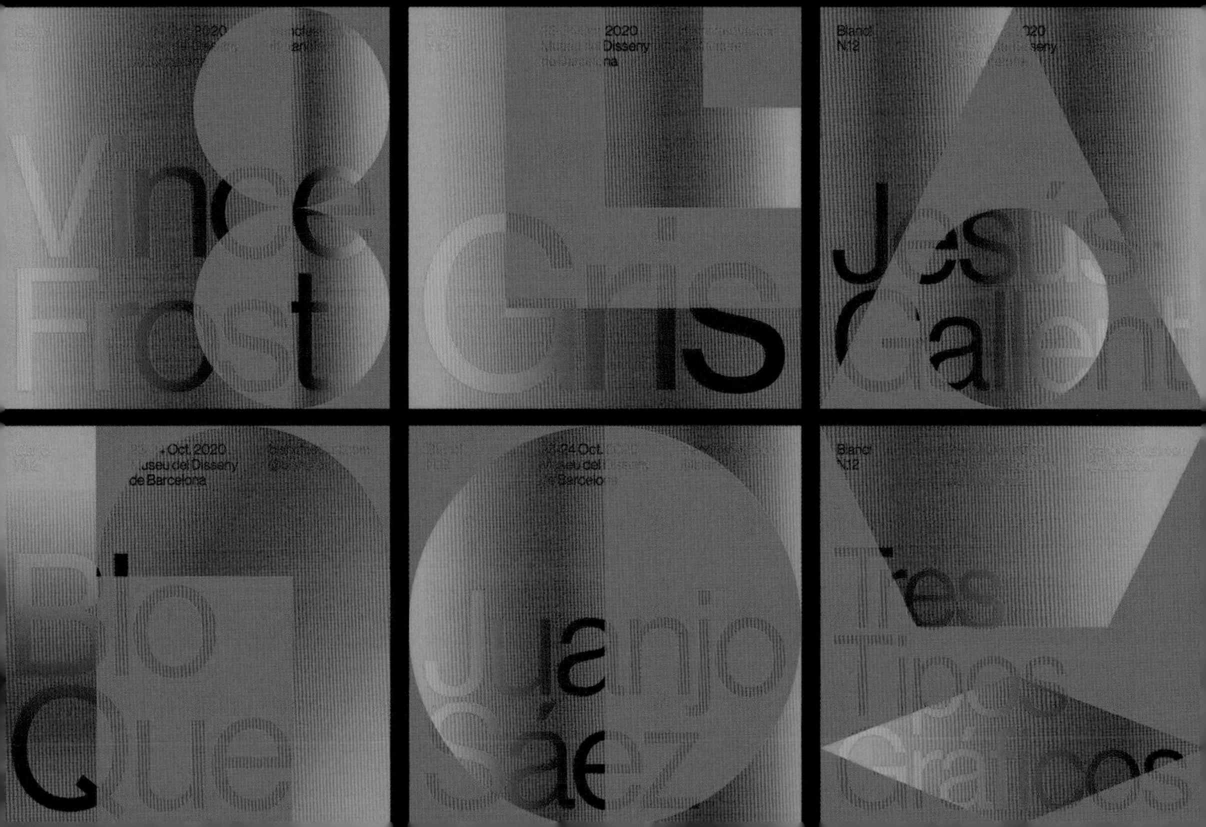

2020

24 Oct. 2020
seu del Disseny
Barcelona

blancfestival.com
@blancfest

ce Frost, Studio Dumbar, Mark Brooks,
za Twins, Anton & Irene, Juanjo Sáez,
, Bendita Gloria, Folch, Toni Miserachs,
nica Rodriguez, Tres Tipos Gráficos,
én Torregrosa, Jesús Gallent,
ilia Tham, Gris, Blo que, Cristina Malet,
eel, Sala Ferusic, Suelasdegoma
ssimo Pignata

Blanc!
N.12
2020

2020

Blanc!
N.12

23-24 Oct. 2020
Museu del Disseny
de Barcelona

blancfestival.com
@blancfest

Vince Frost, Studio Dumbar, Mark Brooks,
Yarza Twins, Anton & Irene, Juanjo Sáez,
Hey, Bendita Gloria, Folch, Toni Miserachs,
Mònica Rodriguez, Tres Tipos Gráficos,
Belén Torregrosa, Jesús Gallent,
Cecilia Tham, Gris, Blo que, Cristina Malet,
B-reel, Sala Ferusic, Suelasdegoma
i Massimo Pignata

Vince F
Yarza T
Hey, Be
Mònica
Belén T
Cecilia
B-reel, S
i Massir

23-24 Oct. 2020
Museu del Disseny de Barcelona

Vince Frost, Studio Dumbar, Mark Brooks, Yarza Tw
Juanjo Sáez, Hey, Bendita Gloria, Folch, Mònica Ro
Toni Miserachs, Tres Tipos Gráficos, Belén Torreg
Cecilia Tham, Blo que, Cristina Malet, B-reel, Sala F
i Massimo Pignata

Blanc!

23-24 Oct. 2020
Museu del Disseny
de Barcelona

Blanc!

23-24
Museu

Vince F
Juanjo
Toni M

N.12
2020

23-24 Oct. 2020
Museu del Disseny de Barcelona

blancfestival.com
@blancfest

Blanc!

Blanc!
N.12

23-24 Oct. 2020
Museu del Disseny
de Barcelona

blancfestival.com
@blancfest

Vince Frost, Studio Dumbar, Mark Brooks,
Yarza Twins, Anton & Irene, Juanjo Sáez,
Hey, Bendita Gloria, Folch, Toni Miserachs,
Mònica Rodriguez, Tres Tipos Gráficos,
Belén Torregrosa, Jesús Gallent,
Cecilia Tham, Gris, Blo que, Cristina Malet,
B-reel, Sala Ferusic, Suelasdegoma
i Massimo Pignata

blancfestival.com
@blancfest

OÖ Kulturquartier

Studio Yukiko → y-u-k-i-k-o.com
In Upper Austria, the OÖ Landes-Kultur GmbH is where the radical and the classical meet. With its numerous museums, permanent and temporary art spaces and educational programs, this important cultural institution maintains collections and permanent exhibitions on nature, culture and art, all housed in varied locations such as the OÖ Kulturquartier. Its contemporary art exhibitions pay special attention to practitioners from the region like Valie Export, while also championing an international array of young artists such as Oli Epp and Anna Ehrenstein.

A sub identity was created for the art quarter, an array of buildings with numerous exhibition spaces, that in a quiet literal way showed a quarter of a circle. This frame is used throughout communication assets, becoming a container for information.

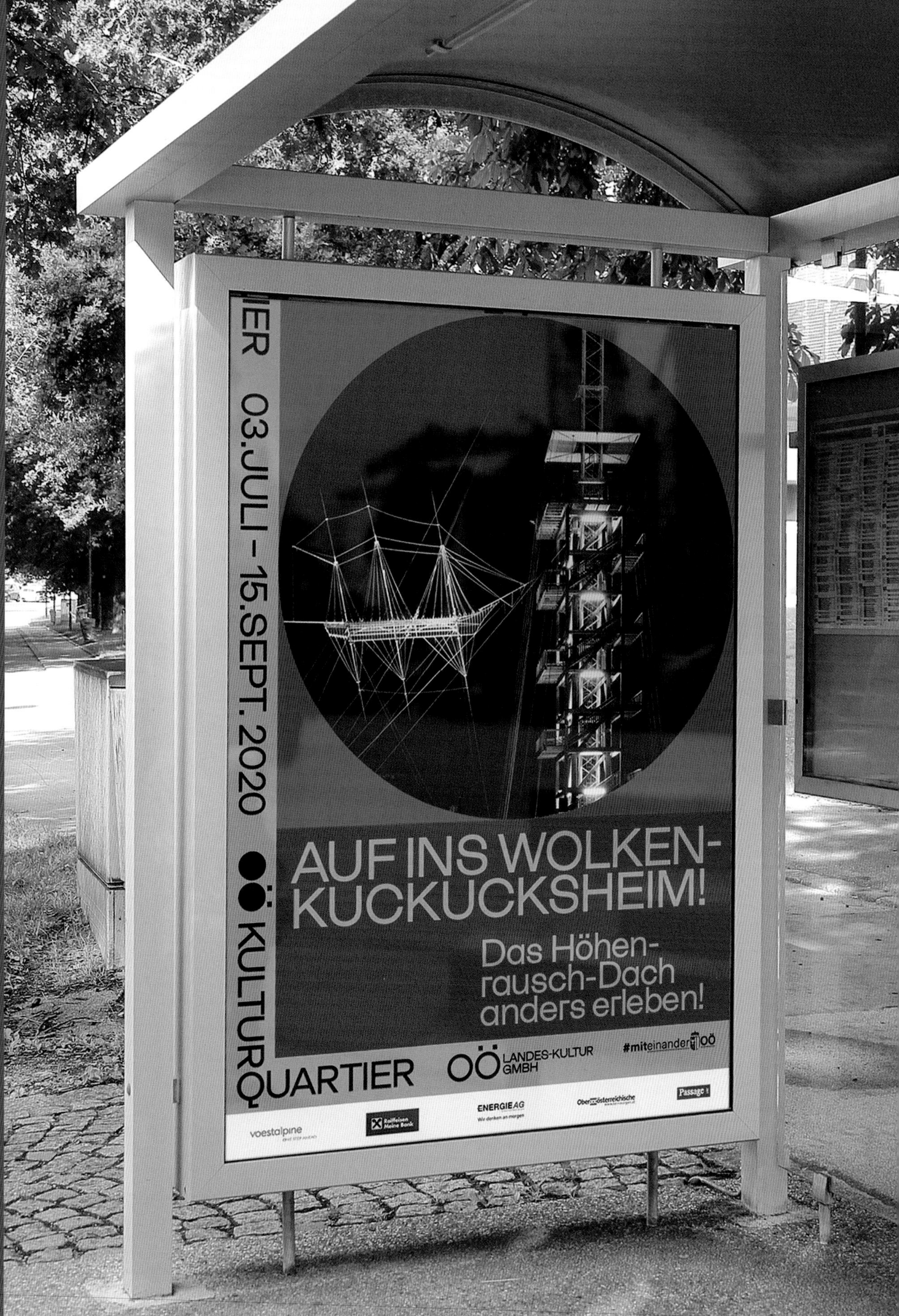

03.JULI – 15.SEPT. 2020
OÖ KULTURQUARTIER
AUF INS WOLKEN-
KUCKUCKSHEIM!
Das Höhen-
rausch-Dach
anders erleben!
OÖ LANDES-KULTUR GMBH
#miteinander OÖ
voestalpine
ENERGIE AG
Wir denken an morgen
Oberösterreichische
Passage

KUNSTKINO PROGRAMM

03.JULI – 15.SEPT. 2020 ●● KULTUR

PROGRAMM 1: HIMMEL
UND HÖLLE | HEAVEN A
AMM 3: BÜHNE DER
STILLE | STAGING SIL

RAMM 2: DIE WELT
KOPF | UPSIDE DO
PROGRAMM 4:
STARRY NIGHT

ROGRAMM 3:
BÜHNE DER
M 5: UND
SIE BEWE

STARRY
NIGHT
M 6:
SONI

SICH

QUARTIER ●● KULTUR

'A sub identity was created for the art quarter, an array of buildings with numerous exhibition spaces, that in a quiet literal way showed a quarter of a circle.'

2nd Encounter in Macao

Untitled Macao → untitledmacao.com

The 2nd 'Encounter in Macao – Arts and Cultural Festival between China and Portuguese-speaking Countries', organised by the Cultural Affairs Bureau, featured six highlights. Namely the 'Macao International Book Fair 2019', the 'Traditional Chinese Strings and Fado concert by the Macao Chinese Orchestra', the 'China and Portuguese-speaking Countries Film Festival', the 'Annual Arts Exhibition between China and Portuguese-speaking Countries', 'Traditional Music and Dance Performance from China and Portuguese-speaking Countries' and 'A Cherished Memory from 1999 – Archives Exhibition in Celebration of the 20th Anniversary of the Return of Macao to the Motherland'.

第二屆 相約澳門 中葡文化藝術節 2019
2ND ENCOUNTER IN MACAO – ARTS AND CULTURAL FESTIVAL BETWEEN CHINA AND PORTUGUESE - SPEAKING COUNTRIES
WWW.ICM.GOV.MO/FCP
Partidas 出国
離境
Departures 출국

二十周年
檔案展
第二屆相約澳門—中葡文化藝術節
2ND ENCOUNTER IN MACAO – ARTS AND CULTURAL FESTIVAL BETWEEN CHINA AND PORTUGUESE-SPEAKING COUNTRIES
澳門國際書展2019
FEIRA INTERNACIONAL DO LIVRO DE MACAU
MACAO INTERNATIONAL BOOK FAIR
7/4-7/7

第二屆 相約澳門
中葡文化藝術節
2019

2019
第二屆相約澳門—中葡文化藝術節
FEIRA INTERNACIONAL DO LIVRO DE MACAU
澳門國際書展
MACAO INTERNATIONAL BOOK FAIR
ROBERTSON
26

第二屆 相約澳門 中葡文化藝術節
澳門中樂團
20:00
7/5

INTERNATIONAL EXHIBITION AREA
This area mainly displays overseas food and wine publications. The exhibitors include a number of publishers from Portuguese-speaking countries and world-famous cookbook publishers, who are ready to establish business relationships regarding copyright trading during the book fair.
READING EXPERIENCE AREA
This area gathers together gastronomy books and related cultural products.
CHEF'S KITCHEN
This area features a scene in the kitchen where Chinese and foreign master chefs offer live cooking demonstrations, which allows viewers to learn, watch and taste the delicacies prepared by the master chefs.
SALON AREA
Seminars on publishing culture, writers' dialogues, book launches, exchange sessions for Chinese and foreign gourmands will be held in the salon area.
107
2nd ENCOUNTER IN MACAO – ARTS AND CULTURAL FESTIVAL BETWEEN CHINA AND PORTUGUESE-SPEAKING COUNTRIES

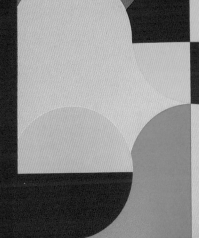

119

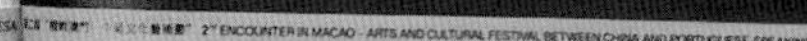

12

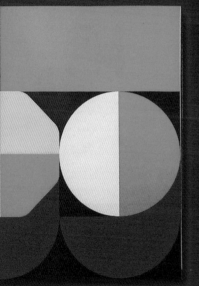

Duane Dalton

Interview 03

Duane Dalton is an Irish graphic designer who specialises in logo design and brand identity systems. Minimalistic qualities are often employed throughout his work to communicate a clear and precise message.

→ duanedalton.com

What is your background and how did you become involved in graphic design?

I'm from Dublin, Ireland but moved to London with my partner about eight years ago now. I didn't really discover graphic design until quite late in my education. I always had a keen interest in art and achieved a degree in that subject. My artwork always embraced a graphic aesthetic, often exploring simple forms and various colour studies. After my art degree I went back to college to study graphic design, or at least what I believed to be graphic design at the time. In my first week in the graphic design course my tutor introduced me to the work of Wim Crouwel and Josef Müller Brockmann. This opened up a whole new world to me, I couldn't believe this type of work existed. It seemed to be something I had been looking for the whole time I was doing my art degree. It was at this moment I knew graphic design was something I felt was worth pursuing. Since then I've been very fortunate to work at some really great studios here in London.

What are you driven by creatively?

Currently, I'm really trying to hone in on my design approach. Over the years I feel I've become more and more critical about my likes and dislikes. So it is a balancing act to filter this into my work. One of my main creative drivers is in embracing self-initiated work. It allows creative freedom to experiment and do what you want. I try not to overthink it and just do some work that I resonate with, and hopefully other people will too.

How important is colour to your work?

Colour can be such a powerful asset. You can communicate so much or so little when it is used right. The possiblities are endless and colour combinations can be so interesting to explore. It's an art form in itself. But like anything, there can be a tendency to rely on your personal likes and dislikes, so it's always good to push beyond your comfort zone and explore other possibilities, especially if a project or client requires a certain outcome.

How do you stop your personal preferences getting in the way of what is required for the client?

I think the right balance is required, in a way the client has hired you because of your preferences and expertise. Use your knowledge as a guide for the deliverables, but trust your preferences. That's where clear communication and discussions with the client are useful to help build trust.

'My artwork always embraced a graphic aesthetic, often exploring simple forms and various colour studies.'

How important is harmony within your colour palettes? Is it always necessary?

This is entirely subjective. Personally, some sort of harmony can work very well and has it uses. But something unexpected and jarring can be far more intriguing and perhaps more memorable.

Do you have a favourite designer or artist for their use of colour and why?

Bridget Riley's artworks are just spectacular in every way, and colour is such a key element in what makes her work so great. Also William Eggleston, the American photographer, who helped pioneer colour photography at a time when black and white was so dominant. How he looked at colour and documented it, I find really interesting.

Do you have a process for selecting a colour palette for a client?

Colour can imbue different meanings, so the sector in which the client/company is involved in can play a significant role. The selection needs to be somewhat appropriate for the given sector. But again, don't be afraid to stray away from what is expected. Sometimes colour selection can be determined by ease of use for the client, or production capabilities for a certain touchpoint. The selection process can vary.

How can an effective colour palette enhance a brand's identity?

Colour is often a more important signifier of a brand than the logo. Personally, I'll recognise a brand's colour scheme from a distance better than the logo. Colour has the ability to work very effectively in non-optimal conditions. For instance, if you're walking amongst a sea of people on Oxford Street and out of the corner of your eye you see a big yellow carrier bag, ah, Selfridges. Colour has the power to become iconic.

138

Yöto Audio Dynamics

Duane Dalton → duanedalton.com

A primary goal set for this project was to create a timeless identity that was inspired by the design sensibilities associated with vintage audio/hi-fi equipment with a contemporary take on it. An unexpected, bright and playful colour palette was an important factor in achieving the desired outcome.

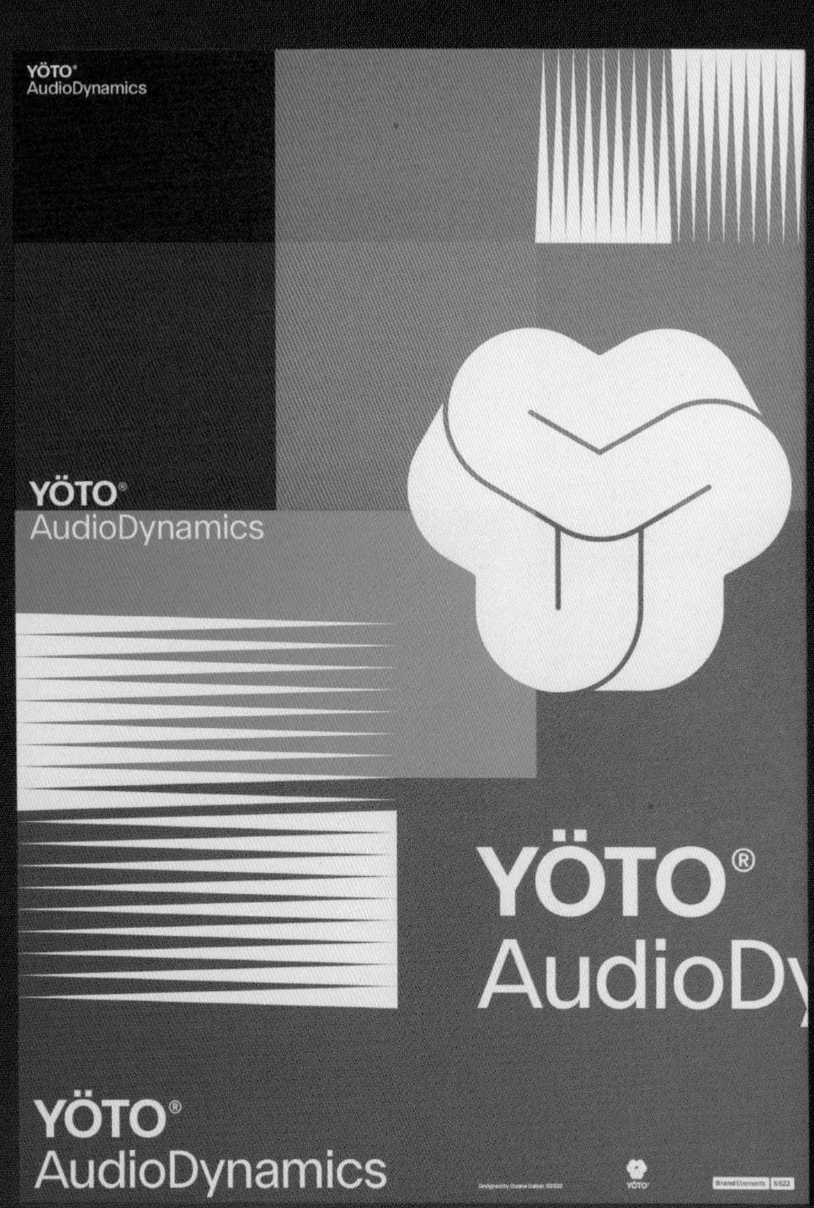

YÖTO°

YÖTO
Elegance
Engineered
YÖTO®
AudioDynamics

YÖTO®

YÖTO®
AudioDynamics

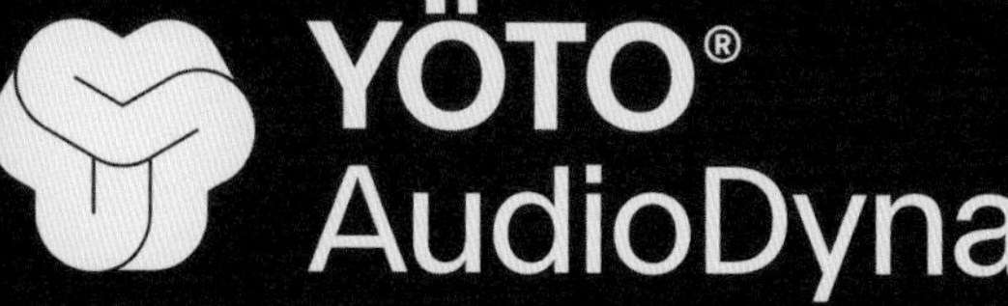
YÖTO®
AudioDynamics

'An unexpected, bright and playful colour palette was an important factor in achieving the desired outcome.'

Perfect Print

Workbyworks Studio → workbyworks.studio
This brand identity design is for Perfect Print, a film development studio based in Shanghai.

Inspired by historical research of optical-related colour palettes used in various brands, a vibrant colour scheme was introduced into the brand.

Combining colours and shapes, the visual system creates a flexible, glitchy pattern of colours, used in all brand applications.

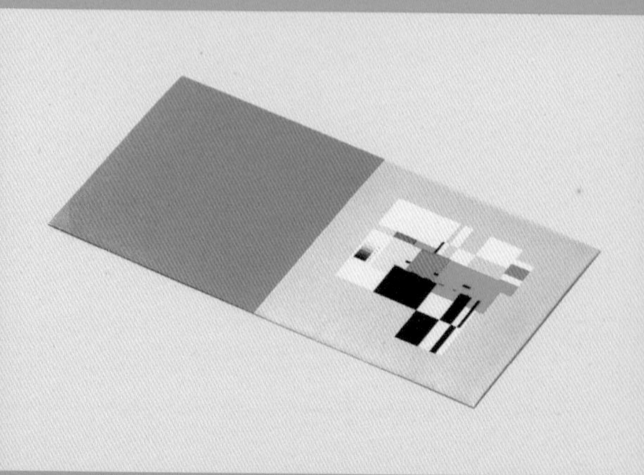

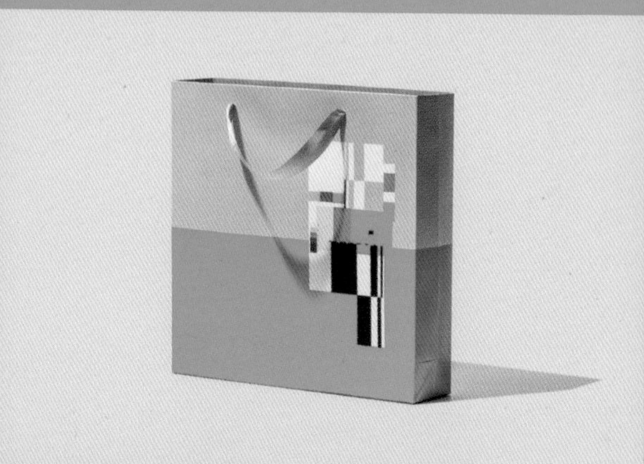

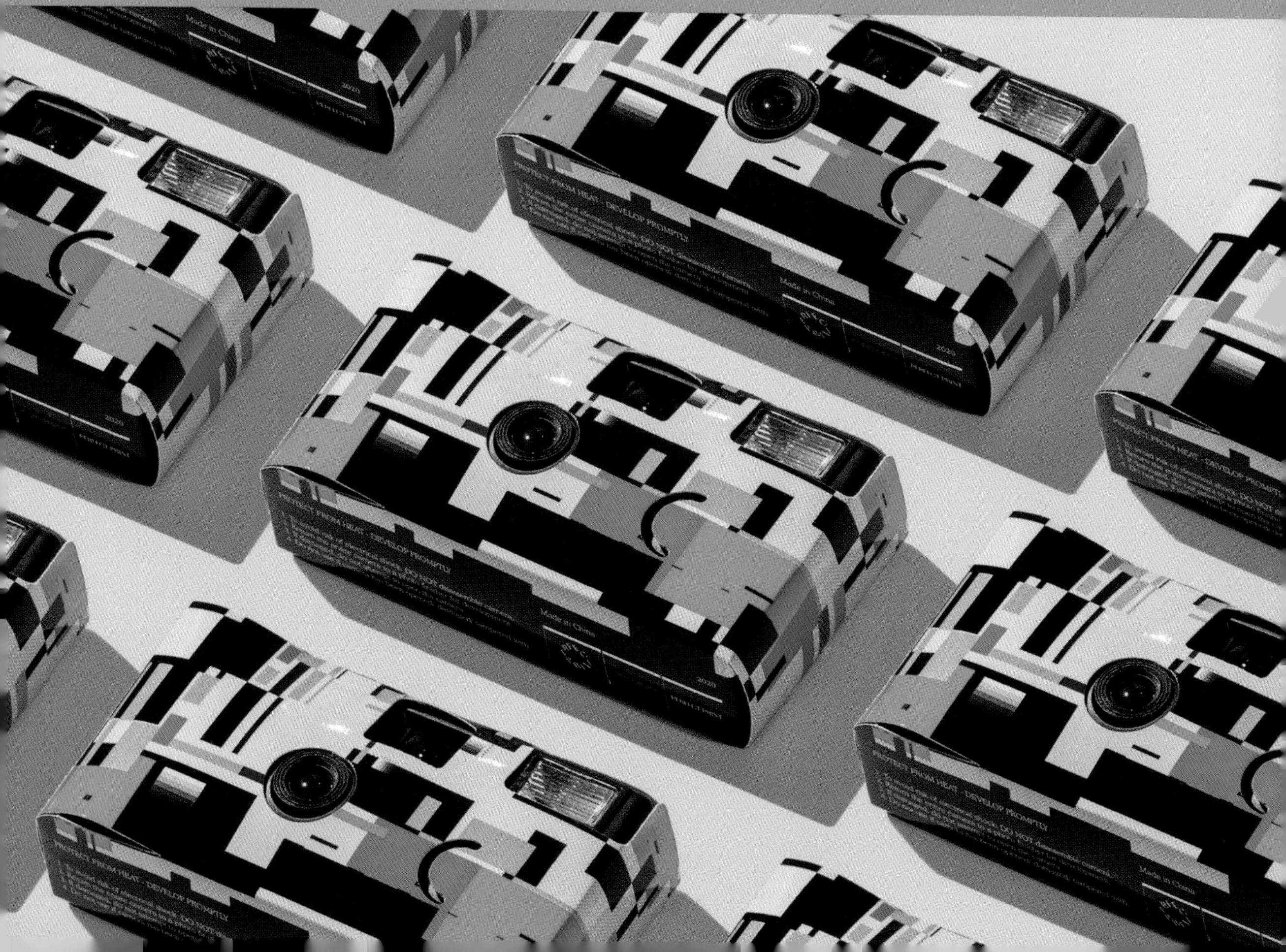

'Combining colours and shapes, the visual system creates a flexible, glitchy pattern of colours, used in all brand applications.'

MACAO DESIGN
澳門設計展
EXHIBITION
講座 SEMINAR

Macao Design Week 2018

Untitled Macao → untitledmacao.com

The theme of Macau Design Week 2018 translated as 'Bring you to the universe to find stories' and the design tried to convey this message.

Visitors were able to walk through a three-dimensional space, from Macao to the rest of the world; climb mountain peaks such as Mount Fuji, chase new experiences, go to the end of the known universe or search for current, topical and influential design works.

MACAO DESIGN WEEK 2018
EXHIBITION
SEMINAR
MASAKI HANAHARA
MACAO DESIGN WEEK
澳門設計周 2018.11.04–11
講座 SEMINAR
設計展 EXHIBITION
MASAKI HANAHARA
DESIGN SEMINAR
設計講座
2018
STAFF
澳門設計周
MACAO DESIGN WEEK
澳門設計展
MACAO DESIGN EXHIBITION
DESIGN EXHIBITION

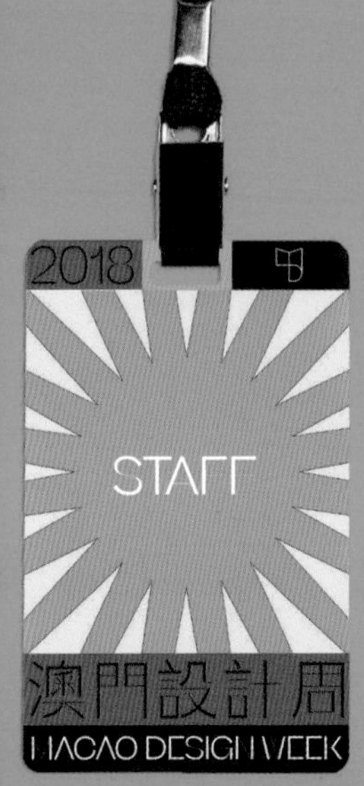
2018
STAFF
澳門設計周
MACAO DESIGN WEEK

2018
STAFF
澳門設計周
MACAO DESIGN WEEK

2018
STAFF
澳門設計周
MACAO DESIGN WEEK

2018
STAFF
澳門設計周
MACAO DESIGN WEEK

MACAO DESIGN WEEK 澳門設計周 2018

EXHIBITION
SEMINAR

MASAKI HANAHARA
EXHIBITION
澳門設計周
MACAO DESIGN WEEK 2018.11.4-11
BOB LEI
SEMINAR
澳門設計周
MACAO DESIGN WEEK 2018.11
AU CHON HIN
SEMINAR
澳門設計周
MACAO DESIGN WEEK 2018.11.4-11
UNTITLED MACA
EXHIBITION
澳門設計周
MACAO DESIGN WEEK 2018.11
UNTITLED MACAO
SEMINAR
澳門設計周
MACAO DESIGN WEEK 2018.11.4-11
SIO KAI TONG
EXHIBITION
澳門設計周
MACAO DESIGN WEEK 2018.11
18.11.4-11
18.11.4-11
18.11.4-11

DIGITAL
設計周
2018.11.4-11
KENNETH HO
SEMINAR
澳門設計周
MACAO DESIGN WEEK
2018.11.4-11
設計周
2018.11.4-11
CLIFFS STUDIO
EXHIBITION
澳門設計周
MACAO DESIGN WEEK
2018.11.4-11
DESIGN
設計周
2018.11.4-11
AMY UN
SEMINAR
澳門設計周
MACAO DESIGN WEEK
2018.11.4-11

SIFF 2020 — A World Different from Yesterday

Ordinary People → ordinarypeople.info

The theme for the 2020 Seoul Independant Film Festival was 'A World Different from Yesterday'.

Design agency Ordinary People wished to convey how, 'reality around us is a superposition of many worlds, with multiple layers of universes based on different perspectives and interpretations'.

To visualise this densely dimensioned world, Ordinary People opted for recursive squares, showing the dimensional expansion of unfolding graphics.

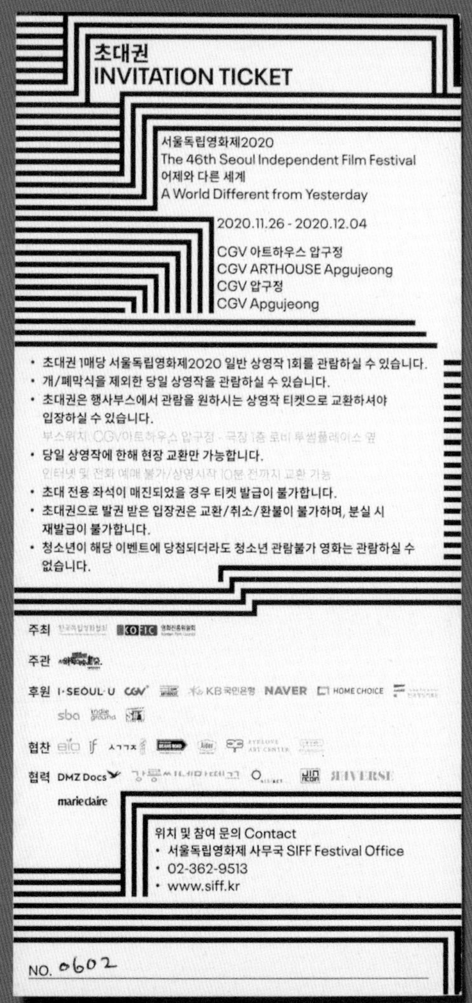

어제와 다른 세계
A WORLD DIFFERENT FROM YESTERDAY
서울독립영화제 2020
The 46th Seoul Independent Film Festival
CGV 아트하우스 압구정
2020.11.26 -12.04
서울獨立映畫祭
서울독립영화제

'To visualise this densely dimensioned world, Ordinary People opted for recursive squares, showing the dimensional expansion of unfolding graphics.'

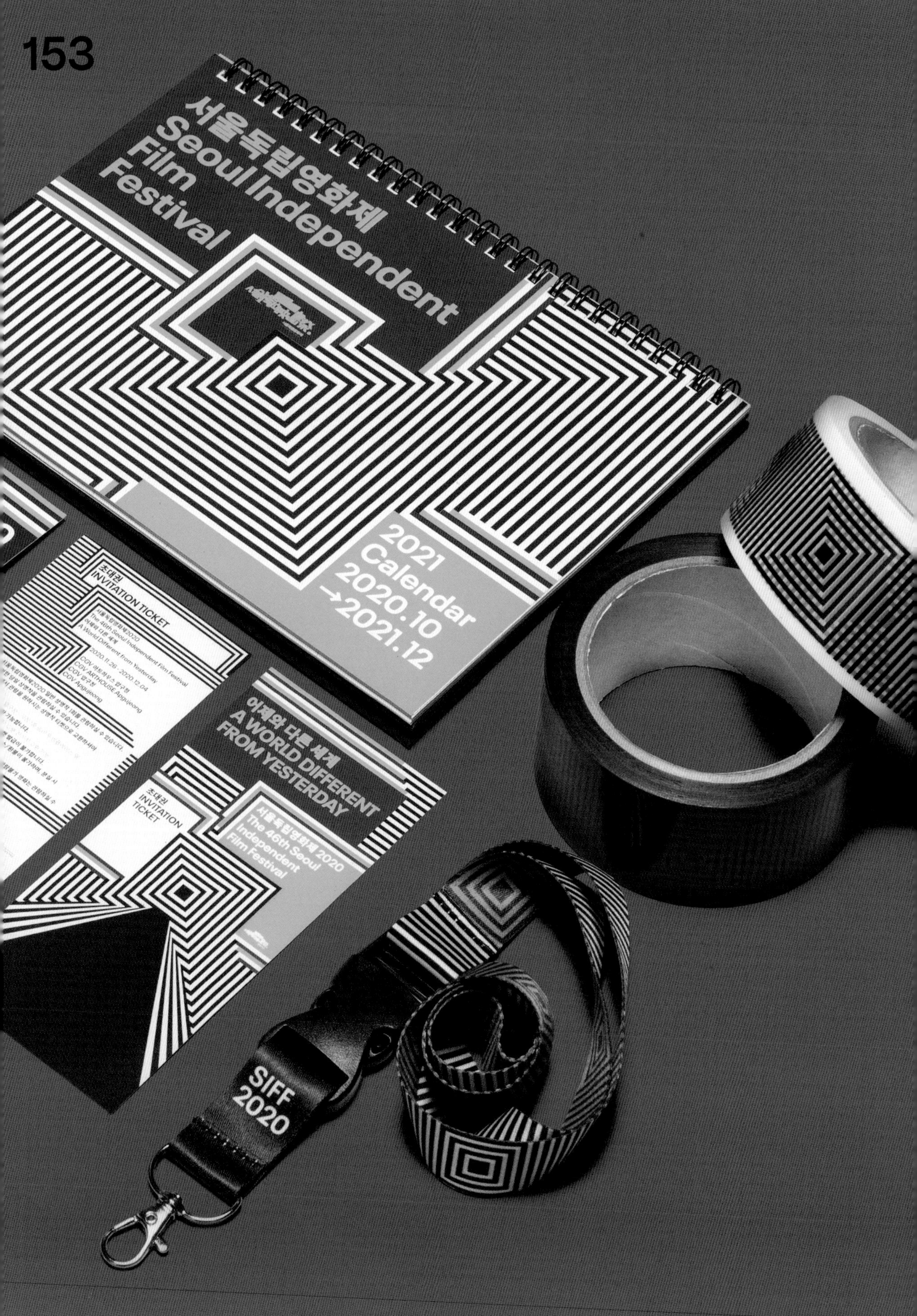
서울독립영화제
Seoul Independent
Film
Festival
2021
Calendar
2020.10
→2021.12
초대권
INVITATION TICKET
어제와 다른 세계
A WORLD DIFFERENT
FROM YESTERDAY
서울독립영화제 2020
The 46th Seoul
Independent
Film Festival
초대권
INVITATION
TICKET
SIFF
2020

ONE
M
STIV

UNSOLICITED OPINIONS PROJECTED IN

FILM SFF.

68

SPOILER-FREE ZONE

REVEALING MAJOR PLOT TWISTS, SURPRISE CAMEOS AND SHOCK ENDINGS IS STRICTLY DISCOURAGED IN THIS AREA.

FILM BRAIN

IF I MISS THE TRAILERS I'M GOING TO HAVE A GENUINE MELTDOWN.

Sydney Film Festival

For The People → forthepeople.agency

Sydney Film Festival brings the anticipation, opinions, quirks and curiosities out from within the theatre, and invites the whole city to be part of and embrace the film festival experience.

During the height of the pandemic, the 2020 season was cancelled and the 2021 season was delayed. Twice. Eventually restrictions were eased, and the perfect opportunity arose to collectively turn off the mute button and allow ourselves to unapologetically revel in the films we love, together.

Sydney Film Festival went into overdrive, leaning into the optimism, colour, and energy that cinema can galvanise in each and every one of us.

SYDNEY FILM FESTIVAL

NOVEMBER 03–21 2021

SPIRITED FILM BANTER BY

SFF

68

COLLECT ALL 200+ FILMS

TICKETS ON SALE NOW AT SFF.ORG.AU

CITY OF SYDNEY

SYDNEY FILM FESTIVAL FAN CLUB MEET: NOV 03–21

SYDNEY FILM FESTIVAL

NOVEMBER 03–21 2021

SPOILER WARNING:

OVERLY-HYPED FILMS FANS OPERATE IN THIS AREA.

SYDNEY FILM FESTIVAL FAN CLUB MEET: NOV 03–21

TICKETS ON SALE NOW AT SFF.ORG.AU

NOVEMBER
03–21
2021
SYDNEY
FILM
FESTIVAL
NOVEMBER
03–21
2021
SPOILERS MONITORED
UNDER THE JURISDICTION OF
S
F
F
68
AFFILIATED WITH
T.F.F.-S.F.F.-A.F.
COLLECT ALL
200+
FILMS
TICKETS ON SALE NOW AT SFF.ORG.AU
CITY OF SYDNEY
SYDNEY
FILM
FESTIVAL
FILM
MEET:
NOV
03–21
NOVEMBER
03–21
2021
SYDNEY
FILM
FESTIVAL
NOVEMBER
03–21
2021
ATTENTION
FELLOW
FILM-
LOVERS:
YES, THAT TWIST WAS
AWESOME. THAT CAMEO —
STILL CAN'T BELIEVE IT. THAT
ENDING — SOOOO GOOD!
BUT, PLEASE, LET'S KEEP
THIS QUEUE SPOILER-FREE.
TICKETS ON SALE NOW AT SFF.ORG.AU
NSW
SYDNEY
CITY OF FILM
CITY OF SYDNEY
SYDNEY
FILM
FESTIVAL

'Sydney Film Festival went into overdrive, leaning into the optimism, colour, and energy that cinema can galvanise in each and every one of us.'

SYDNEY FILM FESTIVAL
NOVEMBER 03–21 2021
LIFE BRAIN
I HATE ADS.
FILM BRAIN
IF I MISS THE TRAILERS I'M GOING TO HAVE A GENUINE MELTDOWN.
AUDIENCE COMMENTARY ON
TICKETS ON SALE NOW AT SFF.ORG.AU
FOYER BUZZ IN
SFFSTEREO
COLLECT ALL 200+ FILMS
LIFE BRAIN
I'M NOT GREAT WITH NAMES.
FILM BRAIN
OOOH, I KNOW THAT STUNT COORDINATOR! AND THAT GAFFER! AND THAT LOCATION SCOUT!
SFF
CULT CLASSICS
LIFE BRAIN
SAVING UP FOR A HOME, BETTER STICK TO THE ESSENTIALS.
FILM BRAIN
30-TICKET SFF FLEXIPASS, THANKS.
UNSOLICITED OPINIONS PROJECTED IN
FILM SFF
CITY OF SYDNEY

HKU Architecture Degree Show 2022

Atelier Avocado → atelieravocado.com

Inspired by the seminal BBC Radio 4 Show, 'Desert Island Discs', HKU Architecture Spring 2022 Public Lecture Series invited five groups of international architects including Go Hasegawa (Japan), Clement Blanchet (France), Hua Li (China), Mark and Jane Burry (Australia) and Alessandra Cianchetta (Italy) to share the buildings they chose 'to bring to the desert island', sharing their inspiration in architecture and how their identity were shaped through their life experience. The poster series visualises the islands by exaggerating their profiles, blurring the definition between natural landscape and architectural formations. The visuals are accentuated by a set of tropical colours which playfully echoes the theme of 'desert islands'.

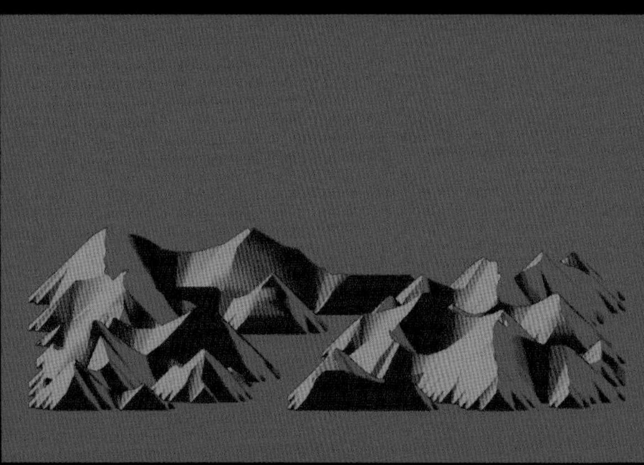

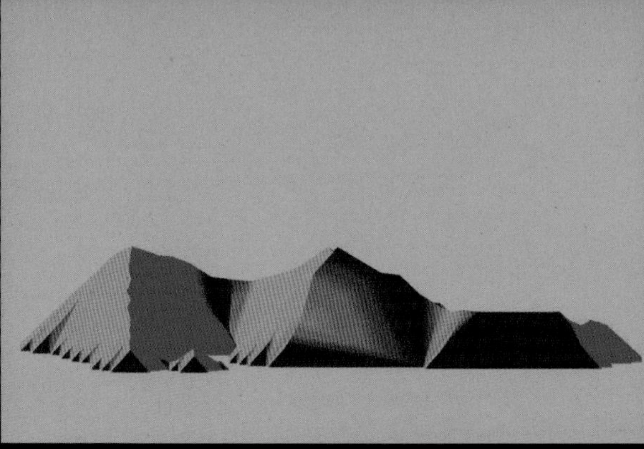

HKU Architecture
Public Lecture Series
Spring 2022
Desert Island
Buildings
香港大學建築學系
2022春季講座
Tuesdays
6–7pm
8 FEB
Go Hasegawa
長谷川豪
22 FEB
Clement
Blanchet
1 MAR
Hua Li
華黎
29 MAR
Mark and
Jane Burry
12 APR
Alessandra
Cianchetta

Go
Hasegawa
長谷川豪
HKU Architecture
Public Lecture Series
Spring 2022
Desert Island
Buildings
香港大學建築學系
2022春季講座
Tuesday
8 FEB
6–7pm

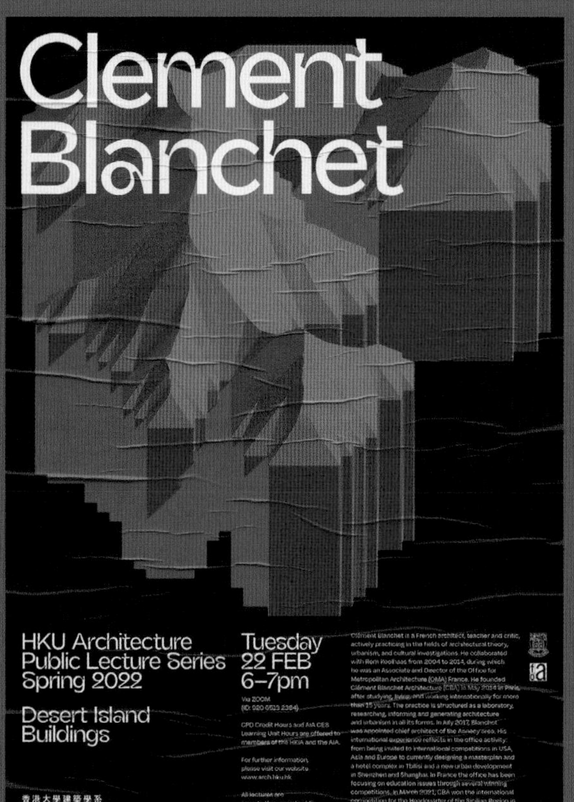

Clement
Blanchet
HKU Architecture
Public Lecture Series
Spring 2022
Desert Island
Buildings
香港大學建築學系
2022春季講座
Tuesday
22 FEB
6–7pm

Hua Li
華黎
HKU Architecture
Public Lecture Series
Spring 2022
Desert Island
Buildings
香港大學建築學系
2022春季講座
Tuesday
1 MAR
6–7pm

Mark and Jane Burry

HKU Architecture
Public Lecture Series
Spring 2022

Desert Island
Buildings

香港大學建築學系
2022春季講座

Tuesday
29 MAR
6–7pm

Via ZOOM
(ID: 920 6513 2384)

CPD Credit Hours and AIA CES Learning Unit Hours are offered to members of the HKIA and the AIA.

For further information, please visit our website www.arch.hku.hk

All lectures are open to the general public.
Enquiry: aleesw@hku.hk

Mark Burry is the Founding Director of Swinburne University of Technology's Smart Cities Research Institute. His role is to lead the development of a whole-of-university research approach to urban futures to help ensure that future cities and regions anticipate and meet the needs of all. He is a practising architect who has published internationally on two main themes: putting theory into practice with regard to procuring 'challenging' architecture; and the life, work and theories of the architect Antoni Gaudí. He has been a Senior Architect to the Sagrada Família Basilica Foundation since 1979, concluding with the completion of the basilica's schematic design and design development of the principal façade (Glory Façade) in 2016. His recent publications include an edited four-volume collection of papers on digital architecture (Routledge – Taylor & Francis, March 2020), and an edition of *Architectural Design* titled 'Urban Futures – Designing the Digitalised City' (Wiley, May/June 2020).

Jane Burry is an architect, Professor and Dean of the School of Design at Swinburne University of Technology. She is the lead author of *The New Mathematics of Architecture* (Thames & Hudson, 2010), editor of *Designing the Dynamic* (Melbourne Books, 2013), co-author of *Prototyping for Architects* (Thames & Hudson, 2016), and has over a hundred other publications. She co-chaired *FABRICATE 2020*, co-edited *Making Resilient Architecture* (UCL Press, 2020), co-curated the 2018 International Exhibition *Dynamics of Air*, and co-directs Smartgeometry. She has practised and taught internationally, including involvement as a project architect in the technical office at Antoni Gaudí's Sagrada Família Basilica with partner Mark Burry. Her recent research investigates architectural geometry and materiality in tandem with rich environmental data gathering to fine-tune the acoustic, thermal and airflow design for high-quality, human-centric environments.

Alessandra Cianchetta

HKU Architecture
Public Lecture Series
Spring 2022

Desert Island Buildings

香港大學建築學系
2022春季講座

**Tuesday
12 APR
6–7pm**

Via ZOOM
(ID: 920 6513 2384)

CPD Credit Hours and AIA CES Learning Unit Hours are offered to members of the HKIA and the AIA.

For further information, please visit our website www.arch.hku.hk

All lectures are open to the general public.
Enquiry: aleesw@hku.hk

Alessandra Cianchetta is an architect and founding partner of AWP AWILDC, an architecture practice based in New York, Paris and London. Born in Italy, she studied architecture at La Sapienza in Rome, ETSA Madrid, and ETSA Barcelona, before setting up AWP in 2008. Her recent projects include Poissy Galore, a museum and observatory set in a park along the Seine River near Paris; the Ten Streets Arts District in Liverpool; Field of Lines, an on-site installation for the Venice Biennale Architettura in 2021; and In-Land living, a series of art barns in Upstate New York. Her projects were nominated for the European Union Prize for Contemporary Architecture – Mies van der Rohe Award in 2009, 2015 and 2016. Her brainchild, Poissy Galore won the ArchiDesignClub Award for the French Cultural Building of the Year in 2018. In addition to practice, Cianchetta has taught architecture and urban design at Cornell University, University of Virginia, Columbia University, The Cooper Union, and The Berlage.

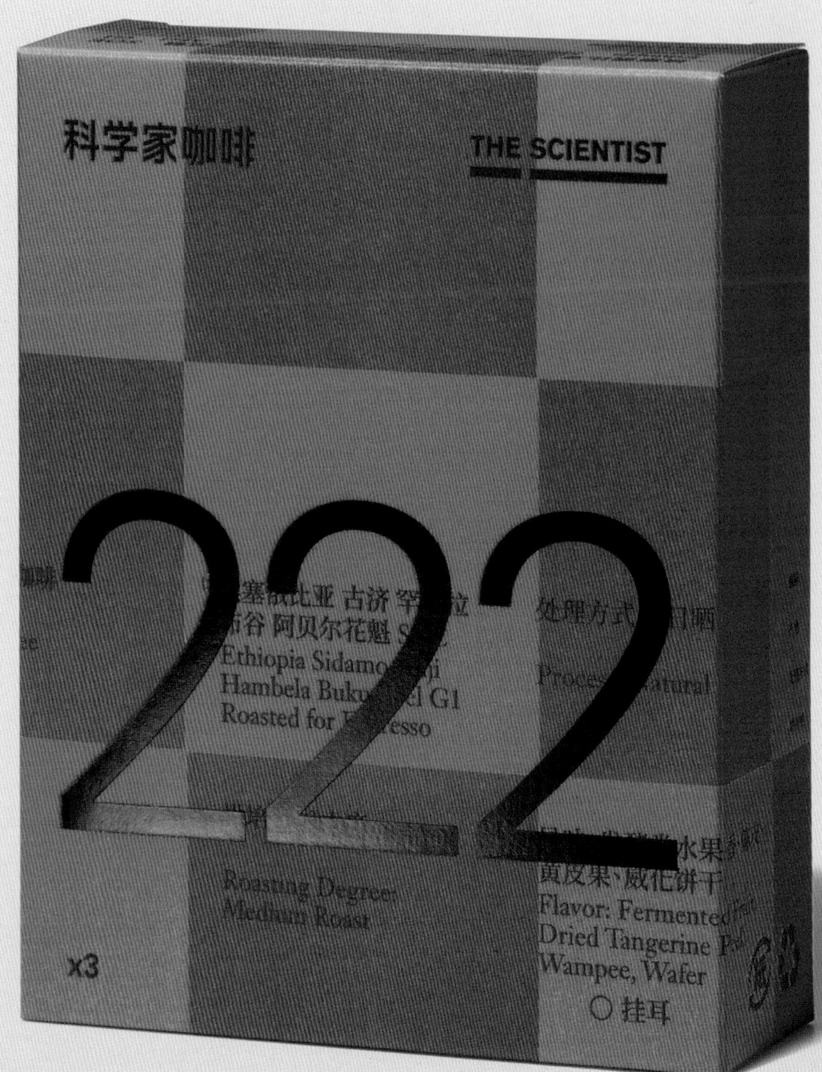

T^2S^2

HDU^{23} Lab → behance.net/hdu23.design

T^2S^2 is the code name of The Scientist Coffee's 2022 New Year season. HDU^{23} Lab wanted to use the number '22' to express their wish to double the good things in the new year.

The visual idea of this season is conveyed by the interaction of square grids that represent a doubling of good luck. The square grids appear in posters, packaging, products and other applications in different proportions, which unify the visual identity of materials.

THE SCIENTIST
THE SCIENTIST

THE SCIENTIST
THE SCIENTIST

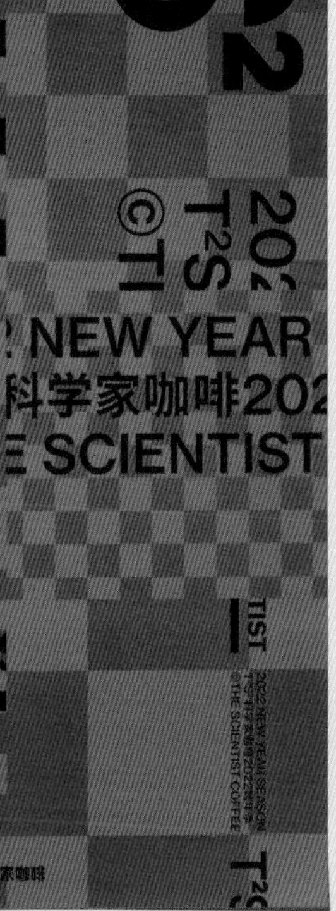
NEW YEAR
SCIENTIST

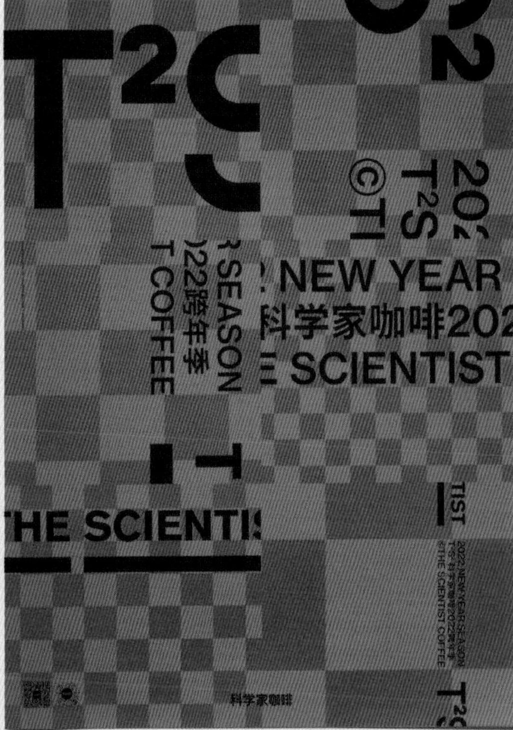
T²S
NEW YEAR
SEASON
22跨年季
T COFFEE
SCIENTIST
2022 NEW YEAR SEASON
T²S 科学家咖啡2022跨年季
©THE SCIENTIST COFFEE
科学家咖啡

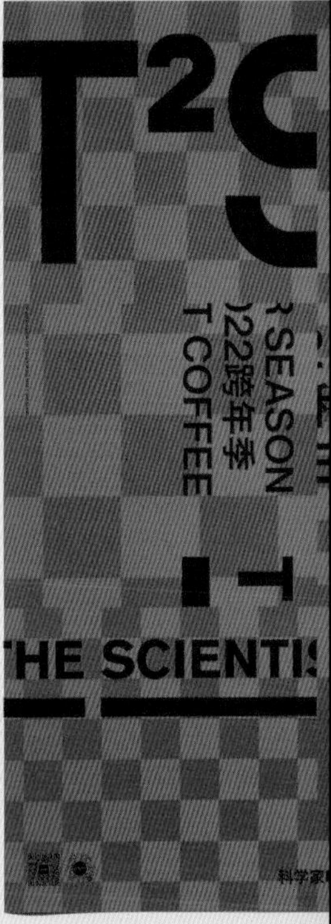
SEASON
22跨年季
T COFFEE

心想事成
BEST
WISHES
T²S²
#T²S² 2022 NEW YEAR SEASON
COPYRIGHT © THE SCIENTIST.
ALL RIGHTS RESERVED.
新年快乐
HAPPY
NEW
YEAR
THE SCIENTIST
万事如意
ALL THE
BEST

科学家咖啡

科学家咖啡
THE SCIENTIST
222
Drip Coffee
Roasting Degree:
Medium Roast
100%
阿拉比卡
咖啡豆
x3

科学家咖啡
THE SCIENTIST
222
Roasting Degree:
Medium Roast
x3

THE SCIENTIST
T²S²
THE SCIENTIST
科学家咖啡202
E SCIENTIST
SCIENTIS
2022 NEW YEAR SEASON
T²S² 科学家咖啡2022跨年季
©THE SCIENTIST COFFEE
科学家咖啡

T²S²
#T²S² 2022 NEW YEAR SEASON
COPYRIGHT © THE SCIENTIST
ALL RIGHTS RESERVED.
THE SCIENTIST

The Davidson Prize

DNCO → dnco.com

Named after the late architectural CGI pioneer Alan Davidson, The Davidson Prize recognises innovative and transformational architecture of the home. Where we live and how we live will only increase in importance over the coming years and DNCO took cues from how the prize shines a light on this under-awarded area of architecture.

Creating a geometric version of this spotlight gives rise to a powerful prismatic graphic language. Much like the nature of our homes which are constantly evolving, it is also a flexible and adaptable system housing typography and imagery, but more importantly, celebrating the people and projects that define the prize.

THE
DAVIDSON
PRIZE
2021
HOME/
WORK

#thedavidsonprize

'Named after the late architectural CGI pioneer Alan Davidson, The Davidson Prize recognises innovative and transformational architecture of the home.'

THE
DAVIDSON
PRIZE

Edinburgh International Film Festival

Touch → thetouchagency.co.uk
As film fanatics, Touch were delighted to be appointed to create the enlightening new identity and campaign for Edinburgh International Film Festival.

Inspired by light beams and cinematic projection, the geometric identity came alive on the big screen through a series of animated idents, while the bold street posters, banners, t-shirts and totes allowed the festival to engage with diverse audiences.

Touch also worked with a team of young people to develop a vibrant sub-brand for EIFF Youth, which was rolled out into signage, posters, tees, and a riso-printed poster/catalogue.

EDINBURGH INTERNATIONAL
FILM FESTIVAL
Think
Gasp
Cheer
Share
Discuss
Debate
Learn
Reflect
edfilmfest.org.uk
#edfilmfest
19–30 June 2019
ED
FILM
FEST
Be Enlightened
19–30 June 2019
Be Enlightened

Lucia Festival

Muttnik → muttnik.it

Lucia Festival is an international program dedicated to listening. Audio stories from all around the world are sought and collected to celebrate the art of storytelling.

For the communication of the 2021 edition, a new graphic system was designed to convey the sensation of acoustic wave distortions.

Round shapes were chosen to express pressures, compressions, decompression and movements. The different images come from the manipulation of circles and were employed in all the communication materials of the festival, to present every single event that took place in special locations in Florence, Italy.

Lucia Festival
10,11,12 dicembre
2021
storie audio dal mondo
ascolti
radio
podcast live
talk
luciafestival.org
Firenze
ON AIR

LUCIA
FESTIVAL

Lucia Festival
10,11,12 dicembre 2021

Firenze

storie audio dal mondo
ascolti
radio
podcast live
talk

Villa Galileo
Kunsthistorisches Institut in Florenz
Orto botanico "Giardino dei Semplici"
The Stellar
The Recovery Plan

progetto grafico: multiuse

un progetto di

Radio Papesse

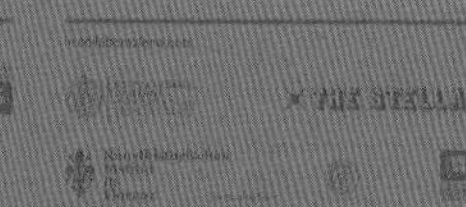

Radio 3

Radio Techetè

mlol

SDIAF

www.luciafestival.org

'For the 2021 edition, a new graphic system was designed to convey the sensation of acoustic wave distortions.'

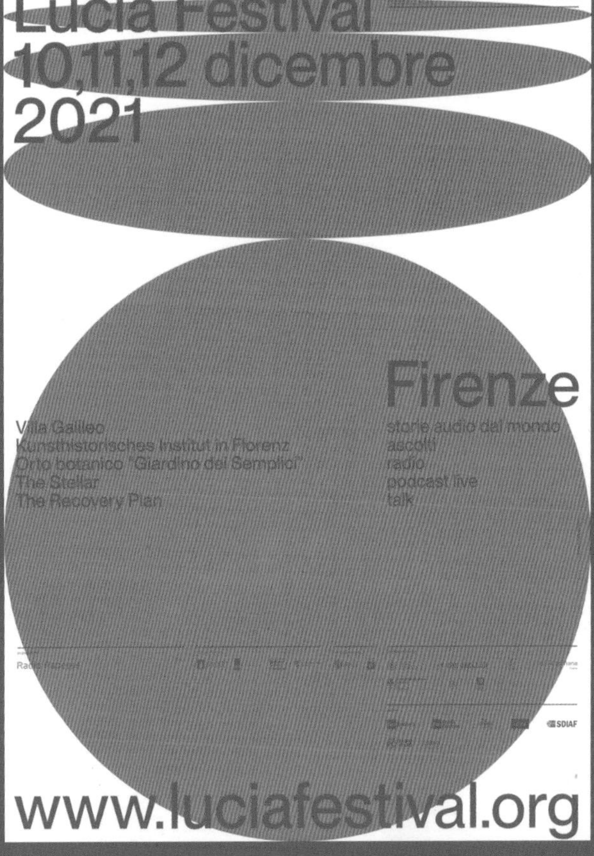

178 LAY—OUT N° 6

My Name is Wendy → mynameiswendy.fr

'LAY—OUT' is a series of artist books curated by the designer Rob Carmichael and it can be purchased via shop.seenstudio.com.

"My Name is Wendy is the artistic and design collaboration of Carole Gautier and Eugénie Favre, whose visual output is immersive, eye-popping and densely layered. They make work that is just as uncompromisingly strange and beautiful when the client is a huge corporation as they do when collaborating with a small cultural organization. For 'LAY—OUT', My Name is Wendy drops the viewer into a world awash with candy-colored gradients, optical dissonance, and fantastical three-dimensional renderings. The pages seem to physically vibrate with energy as one's eyes devour their compositions. The effect is hypnotizing, meditative, and joyous." Rob Carmichael

'The pages seem to physically vibrate with energy as one's eyes devour their compositions.'

Style, colors, ligns
matter, reflect

ready-to-wear
collection
a.z

ready

AME IS WENDY STUDIO

MY NAME IS WENDY STUDIO
2021

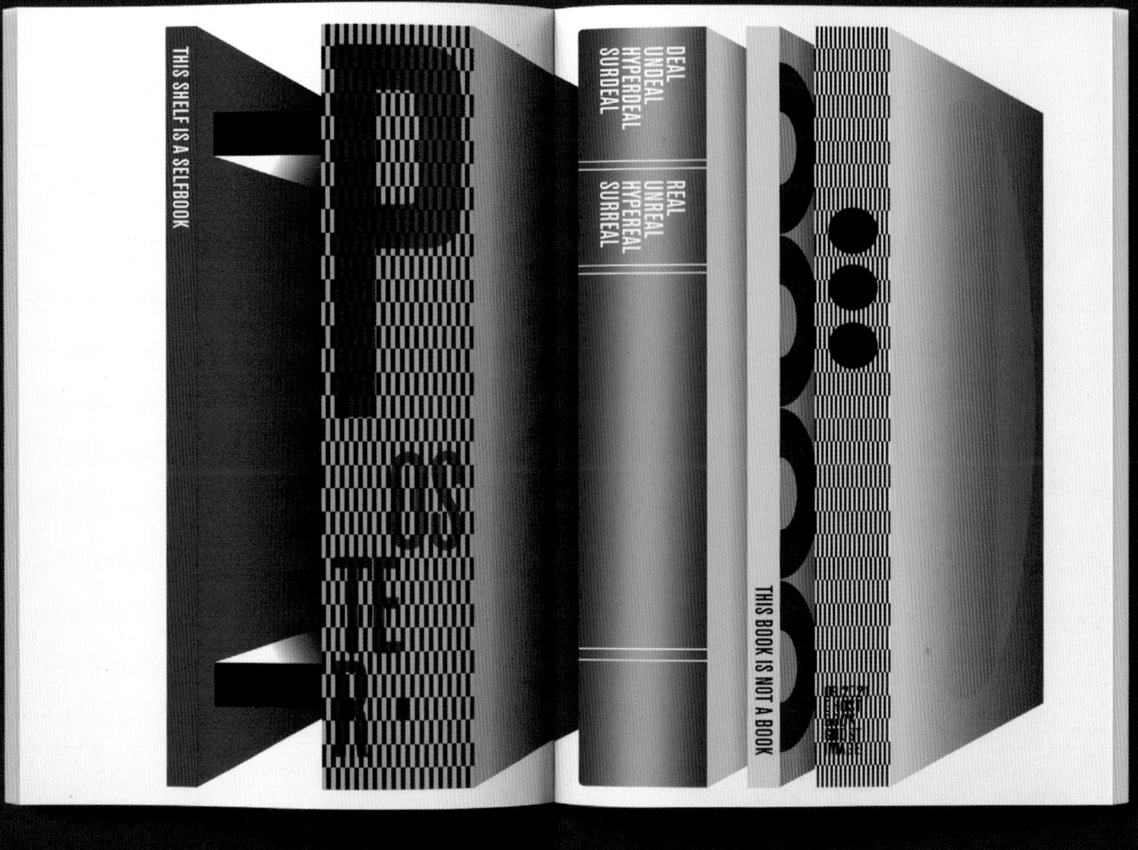

THIS SHELF IS A SELFBOOK

P
OS
TE
R.

DEAL
UNDEAL
HYPERDEAL
SURDEAL

REAL
UNREAL
HYPERREAL
SURREAL

THIS BOOK IS NOT A BOOK

BOOSTER POSTER
STUDIO MY NAME IS WENDY

BOOSTER POSTER
STUDIO MY NAME IS WENDY

BOOSTER POSTER
STUDIO MY NAME IS WENDY

BOOSTER POSTER
STUDIO MY NAME IS WENDY

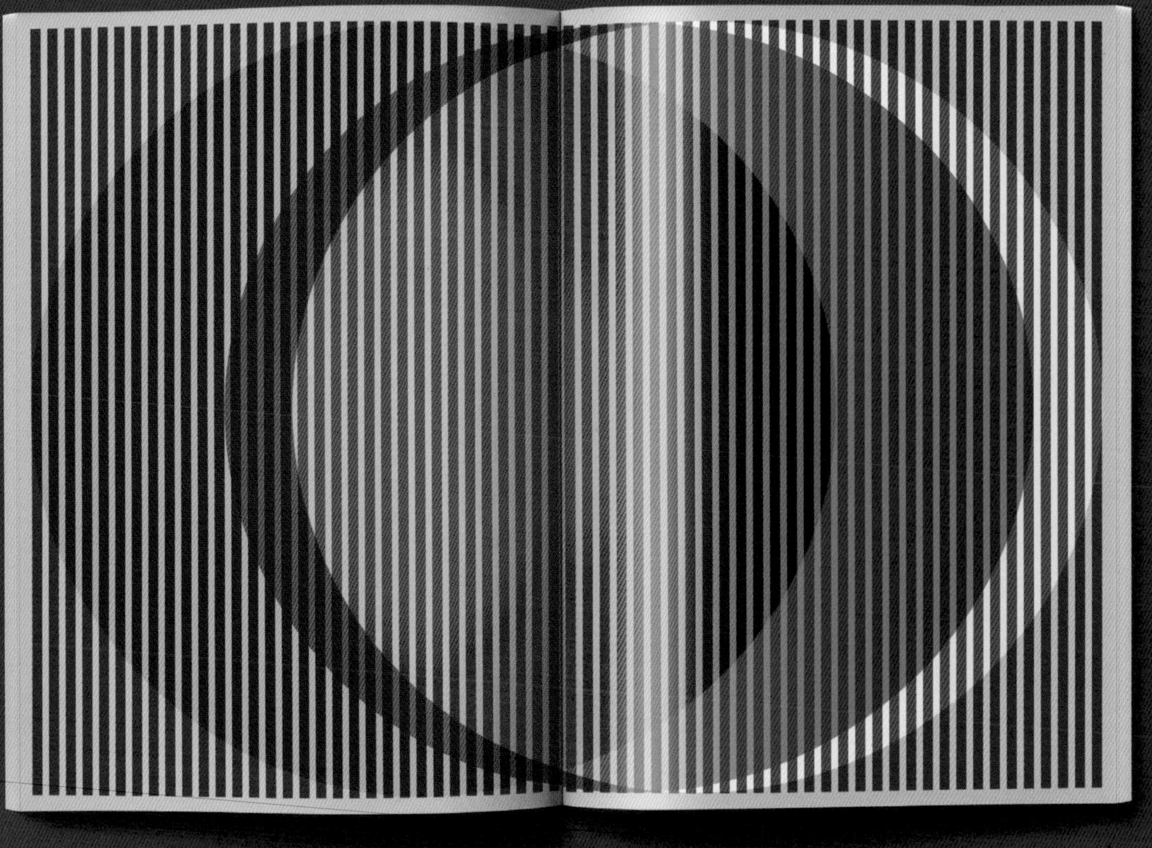

FICHIER CMJN
DIVISÉ EN 4 COUCHES
ET TRAMÉ

GRIS, BITMAP, TRAME DE DEMI-TEINTES
COULEURS INDEXÉES

PHOTO-ÉMULSION

TEMPS
TROP COURT : ÉCRAN SOUS-EXPOSÉ
TROP LONG : ÉCRAN SUR-EXPOSÉ

PHOTO-ÉMULSION
LES NOIRS DOIVENT ÊTRE OPAQUES POUR BLOQUER LA LUMIÈRE

INSOLATION DE L'ÉCRAN
MOUSSE ÉCRAN VITRE
LAMPE AU-DESSUS SUR UN PORTIQUE

TRAME
MAILLE DE LA SOIE
- CADRE 120 POUR 60 DE LINÉATURE
- C'EST À DIRE RAPPORT ENTRE LPI DPI
(DOTS PER INCH)

TYPON
(TRANSPARENT)
VISUEL TIRÉ SUR PAPIER
CALQUE OU TRANSPARENT

IMPRESSION
QUE L'ENCRE PASSE ET APPARAISSE
SUR LE PAPIER.

PREMIER COUP D'ENCRE / DEUXIÈME COUP D'ENCRE
AFIN DE DÉGAGER L'IMAGE EN LA RAMENANT VERS
SOI, EN INCLINANT LA RACLE

Nike NBG

Specht Studio → spechtstudio.com
Stephanie Specht was asked by Enjoy The Weather (Portland) to create affirmation visuals for @nbg.nike (NOTHING BUT GOLD) by Nike – a new kind of shopping app dedicated to sport, style, and self-care for girls who 'Just Do It' their own way.

The app was designed and developed by Enjoy The Weather. It was running in private beta (a.k.a. super-secret-stealth mode), and they wanted people to build with them. The only given assets were dimensions, typography (Future Nike) and the slogans. All produced in the first six months of 2021. Specht developed a simple style with a flashy colour palette so it gained enough attention when people were scrolling through their feed.

YOU'RE
CAPABLE
OF
GREAT
NESS
NbG

NbG
BOUNCE
the harder
the fall
the higher
the bounce

ALL
WE
NbG
HAVE
IS
NOW

YOU
NbG
DESERVE
A
REST

MAKE TIME
FOR YOURSELF
NbG

'Specht developed a simple style with a flashy colour palette so it gained enough attention when people were scrolling through their feed.'

Shenzhen Fringe Festival 2021

Untitled Macao → untitledmacao.com
The first letter of 'Fringe' is used as an inspiration, and further developed into different 'F' letters with various shapes and attitudes. They each contain a pair of abstract and exaggerated eyes which represent the perspectives of participants. Every pair of eyes will discover art and culture that are hidden in the city.

The visual design of Shenzhen Fringe Festival 2021 centered around typography. Untitled Macao hoped to bring out the diversity and uniqueness of art and performance offered around the city by the Festival.

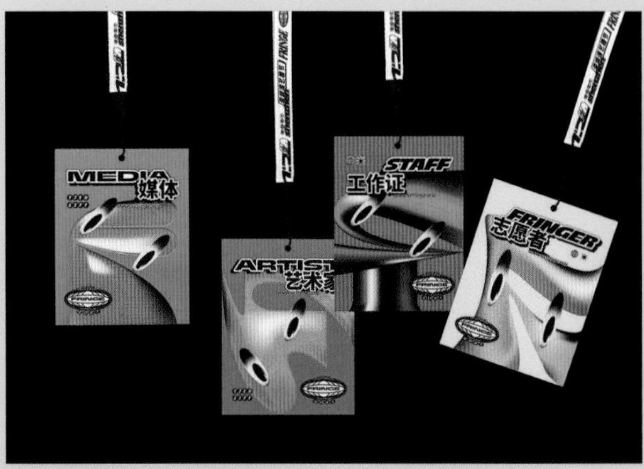

shenzhen
FRINGE
festival
2021
食脑花与乐队
ADOGANDBAND
Quintet
ADOGANDBAND人声五重奏

Shenzhen
FRINGE
深圳湾
festival
www.szfringe.org
2021
Fringe the city
全城艺穗
艺穗节
Nanshan District, Shenzhen
深圳市 南山区
11
10/21
wed
sun
ARTIST 艺术家
STAFF 工作证
MEDIA 媒体

FRINGE
12th
Shenzhen
FRINGE
festival
深圳湾
www.szfringe.org
2021
Fringe the city
全城艺穗
艺穗节
Nanshan District Shenzhen
深圳市南山区
11
10/21
Wed Sun
ORGANIZER
CO-ORGANIZER
STAGE
LIVE

190

Take Care

Andrej & Andrej → andrejandrej.com
Take Care is a publication for the collective exhibition of Generation Y or millennials entitled 'Y'. Millenials are stereotyped for their indecision, instability, laziness, or outright inability to manage basic activities and meet deadlines – the generation of TV screens and smartphones.

Therefore, the publication is impractically big, the texts are laid out along the pages from top to bottom to mimic social media's 'infinite scrolls' and the art works depicted in the publication are accompanied with similar ones generated by a Google image search to symbolise the information-overloaded era we live in.

Graphic Design: David Kalata
Consultant: Palo Bálik

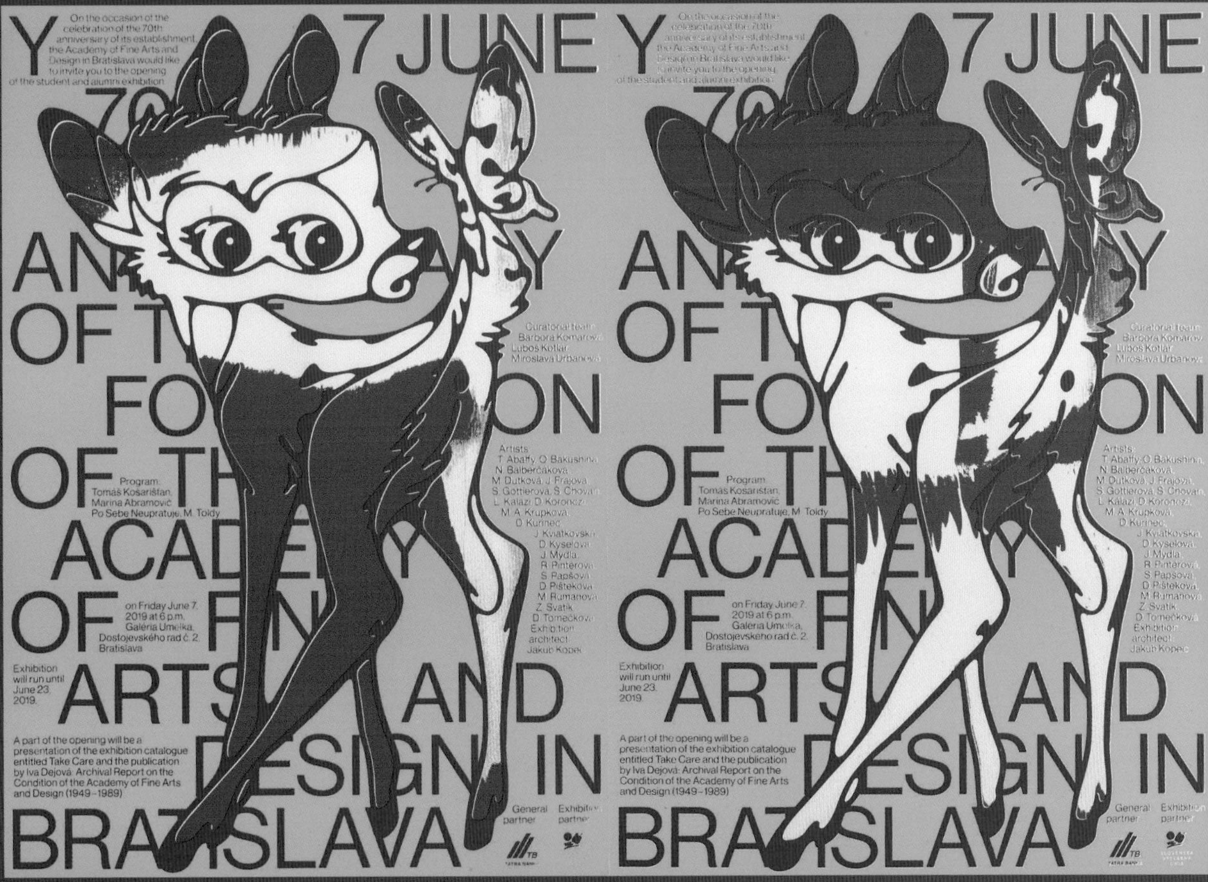

7 JUNE
On the occasion of the celebration of the 70th anniversary of its establishment, the Academy of Fine Arts and Design in Bratislava would like to invite you to the opening of the student and alumni exhibition
Curatorial team: Barbora Komarová, Luboš Kotlár, Miroslava Urbanová
Program: Tomáš Kosarištan, Marina Abramovič, Po Sebe Neupratuje, M. Toldy
Artists: T. Abaffy, O. Bakushina, N. Balberčáková, M. Dutková, J. Frajová, S. Gottierová, S. Chovan, L. Kalazi, D. Koroncz, M. A. Krupková, D. Kurinec, J. Kviatkovski, D. Kyselová, J. Mydla, R. Pinterová, S. Papšová, D. Pišteková, M. Rumanová, Z. Svatik, D. Tomečková
Exhibition architect: Jakub Kopec
on Friday June 7, 2019 at 6 p.m. Galéria Umelka, Dostojevského rad č. 2, Bratislava
Exhibition will run until June 23, 2019.
A part of the opening will be a presentation of the exhibition catalogue entitled Take Care and the publication by Iva Dejová: Archival Report on the Condition of the Academy of Fine Arts and Design (1949–1989)
General partner
Exhibition partner 
DESIGN IN
umení v Bratislave bola založená v roku 1949
politicko-spoločenskom usporiadaní

192 Kappa Sportswear Fashion Show Identity 22SS

Workbyworks Studio → workbyworks.studio
For this show identity, designed for Kappa China, the idea was to explore a new dimension of the beloved Kappa Omini logo heritage, by expanding the Omini system into a spectrum of logos, types and graphics.

KAPPA
Kappa
Authentic Sportswear Brand
Since 1967
1967
KA
1967
Kappa
1967
Kappa
Kappa
Kappa
Kappa
Kappa
1967
KAPPA

KAPPA
1967
KA
Kappa
1967
Kappa
1967
Kappa
Authentic Sportswear Brand
Since 1967
KAPPA
1967

KAPPA
KAPPA
Kappa
Kappa
Kappa
1967
1967
Kappa

KAPPA
Kappa
KAPPA
KAPPA
Kappa
AUTHENTIC
SPORTSWEAR BRAND
SINCE 1967
1967
KA
1967
Kappa
Kappa
1967
Kappa

1967
KA

1967
KA

1967
KA

1967

1967

Kappa

1967

Kappa
1967

Kappa
1967

Authentic
Sportswear Brand
Since 1967
1967

Kappa
1967

Kappa
1967

Kappa
1967

1967
1967
1967
1967
1967
1967
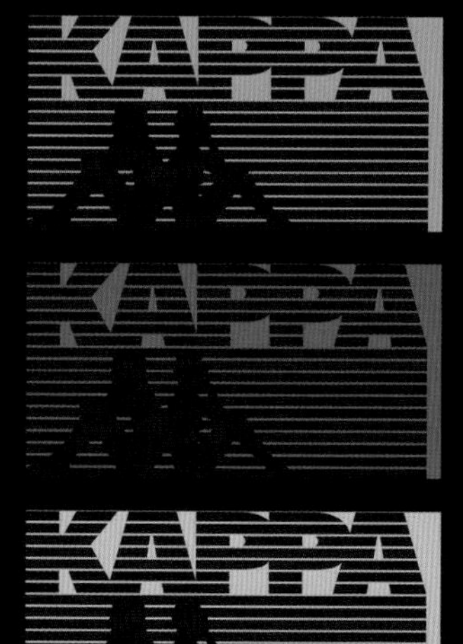
KAPPA
KAPPA

KAPPA

Kappa

'The idea was to explore a new dimension of the beloved Kappa Omini logo heritage.'

1967
Authentic
Sportswear Brand
Since 1967
1967
Authentic
Sportswear Brand
Since 1967
1967
1967
1967
1967
Kappa
AUTHENTIC
SPORTSWEAR BRAND
SINCE 1967
Kappa
AUTHENTIC
SPORTSWEAR BRAND
SINCE 1967
Through a divine simulation of paradigms, hyperreality arises from reality. It is not a game of imitation, nor one of duplication. Rather, it reassembles the familiar and the emblematic in an attempt to supersede the real. It is constituted of matrices, memory banks and command models, a practice that engenders all phenomena in our age. From the iconic black and white, the glorious red and black, to the signature azzurro, this season's color codes refer back to Kappa's vintage football kits. Traveling from the futuristic outlook of the last collection, we now arrive at an aesthetic middle ground between the nostalgic and the hyperreal, where a sense of community and belonging can be found. Athleticism is our destination. Hop on board. Kappa is about to take off.

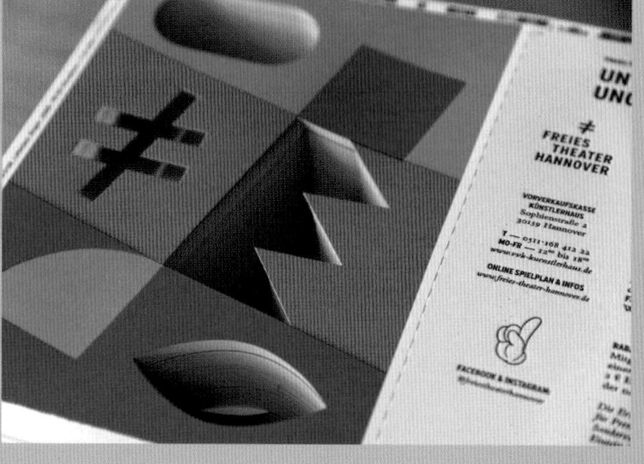

Freies Theater Hannover

Bureau Hardy Seiler → hardyseiler.de
This publication is for Freies Theater Hannover. Inspired by their logo, Bureau Hardy Seiler chose a binding of two ribbons, in combination with a diagonal cutout, for the cover.

Inside you can find information about the different theatres on separate cards, allowing for the removal of theatres or the ability to add new ones. The first card is a special one combining different Pantone colours, papers and structures.

12'13'01'14
SPIELPLAN

FREIES
THEATER
HANNOVER

BUREAU HARDY SEILER & CREATED BY MONKEYS
SPIELPLAN
≠
FREIES
THEATER
HANNOVER